The Wife OF GOD

Fresh Revelation on the Bride of Christ

H. PITTS EVANS

Endorsements

"Pastor Pitts Evans is a gifted teacher and author. In *The Wife of God*, you will hear the voice of the Bridegroom calling you deeper into His heart. Through personal stories, insight from little-known Jewish customs, and powerful words from Scripture, you will receive a fresh revelation of the incredible privilege it is to be part of the Bride of Christ. You will see the Scriptures through a new lens and fall in love with Jesus all over again. I highly recommend this life-changing book."

Evangelist Daniel Kolenda

President and CEO–Christ for All Nations (CfaN)

Ministry offices in nations around the world

"This book touched my heart. I felt like I was touching something of the very 'fabric' of life itself. A story is told of a man walking alongside a river late one evening, when he kicks a small pouch. He picks it up, and it feels like it is filled with small rocks. It is dark, and he cannot see what is inside. He puts his hand in, feels the stones and assumes they are worthless.

To entertain himself as he walks, he throws the 'stones' into the water to hear the sound of the splash. When he gets to his destination and there is some light, he opens the now nearly empty pouch and discovers that what he was so easily discarding was not worthless, small rocks, but various kinds of precious gems and diamonds.

How easy it is for us to discard what might come to us in a small pouch, and to simply dismiss its contents. You have in your hand a pouch of precious gems. They reflect the heart of a man whose spiritual journey I have had the pleasure of joining and influencing. Here, he shares some of the various 'pouches' he has found. He has never discarded their contents blithely, but has valued everything those 'precious gems' have opened for him.

These 'gems' call for us to understand how beloved we are and how intently God wants to deepen His 'husbandly' relationship with us and ultimately and eternally 'marry us.' As you receive the revelation contained in these pages, your life 'in the Spirit' can go to heights and depths you have never yet experienced. This is my prayer for you and for myself!"

Dr. Howard Morgan

Founder and Director-KMI & HMM

Offices in United Kingdom and USA

"The theme of God's desire to have a relationship with humanity, clearly has a primary role in the Bible. In *The Wife of God*, Pitts Evans does an incredible job laying out this truth! While following solid Biblical interpretive criticism, this book brings to light the reality of a glorious, Divine love story, causing a deep burning within to enjoy the benefits of being the Bride of our majestic and passionate Bridegroom, Jesus Christ. If you desire to grow deeper in intimacy with the Lord and want a fuller revelation of His love toward us, then take the time to read and experience the truths of this wonderful book."

Keith Collins

Director–FIRE School of Ministry

Lead Pastor–FIRE Church

Founder and President–Generation Impact

"As a protégé of Dr. H. Pitts Evans, I am honored to write this endorsement for his book, *The Wife of God*. My relationship with Dr. Evans has spanned nearly 14 years, beginning in December of 2002, when he was used by God to open my eyes to fresh revelations concerning angelic visitations. Since that time, I have personally known him to be one of the most outstanding Bible scholars of this generation. I've also noted that he has been gifted with a very strong Apostolic anointing.

There have been few books written in the past 25 years that will have as great an impact upon the Church and the Kingdom of God as Dr. Evans' *The Wife of God*. This book reminds the Church of God's eternal purpose for mankind and how He, as our Bridegroom, eternally yearns for a deeper and more intimate relationship with us. This book's pages are life changing, its contents are restorative, and all its images and illustrations are strategically written to bring the Church (the Bride) back into close intimacy with her Husband (Jesus Christ). I encourage every Kingdom-minded believer to study and fully apply the revelations contained in this book."

Rev. Dr. Patrick George, Mwac, PhD, D.Ed, (D.Min)
Snr. Clergy–Gethsemane Evangelical Ministry, International
President–Royal College of Theology & Administration
Deputy Chaplain Commandant General–UCCRM
Offices in Sierra Leone, Liberia and Guinea

"Pitts takes us on a spiritual journey that you will enjoy as you read. This book will stimulate your heart and help you become more intimately acquainted with our Beloved. His work validates that this love affair with our God is forever and for everyone that says yes to the King."

Pastor/Director Karen Dunham
Living Bread International Church
Offices in Jerusalem, Jericho, the Gaza Strip and USA

"Pitts Evans is a dear friend of mine. He spent a month with us at Love-n-Care Ministries in India, working on the manuscript of this book. Pitts' love for Jesus is contagious, his passion for Christ is astounding, and his deep relationship with the Savior is profound. This book is the combination of all these three. I have yet to see a man as Kingdom-oriented as he, who has given himself completely to God's plans and purposes in and through his life. His deep study on the Bride of Christ will definitely bless you. I know you will be inspired to love the Lord more than ever before. I highly recommend this book."

Pastor Yesupadam Paidipamula

Founder and President–Love-n-Care Ministries International

Offices in India, Germany, USA and Madagascar

"This is a great book, and I'm thankful that Pastor Pitts Evans wrote it. The continuous reference of Christ as the 'Bridegroom' and mankind as the 'Bride' or 'wife' can be found interwoven throughout the Bible. This constant theme of Bride and Bridegroom is rarely, if ever, tackled and explained in depth. In his new book, Pitts takes on this gargantuan and daunting task of examining the many examples, methodically taking them apart one by one, and exploring them from every angle.

Pitts speaks with a pastor's heart as he takes the reader from a mere cognitive knowledge of marriage into a deeper level of intimacy, love, and even romance, to better understand the unknown relationship between God and man. The new understanding and revelation of love can stir powerful emotions.

In a day when marriage and love have been perverted and twisted by secularism, the revelation presented in *The Wife of God* is full of gems that will re-awaken our desire for intimacy with Jesus Christ."

Eugene Bach–Back to Jerusalem

Eugene leads the Chinese mission movement called Back to Jerusalem, which provides essential support for Chinese missionaries in Africa, Asia, and the Middle East. He also has written many books about the underground church in China, North Korea, and Iran.

DEDICATION AND THANKS

This book is dedicated to my wife Mary C. Evans and our three amazing children, Joseph Guest, Courtney Elizabeth and Rachael Marie Evans. I also dedicate this book to our wonderful daughter-in-law Kristi Haring Evans and our five grandchildren, Arabelle, Niko, Ivy, Moses and Unity. Mary, thank you for your love and constant support. I'm eternally grateful that you agreed to be my wife. Thank you for never giving up on me. I love you more today than I did the day I married you. You taught me how to enjoy a relationship with a family, and by extension, with the family of God. May we all serve Jesus together, forever.

Thanks to the Leadership Team, and our entire church family at Whole Word Fellowship. You've prayed for me and graciously listened to endless messages about the Bride of Christ.

Special appreciation and thanks to Pastor's Seymour and Jurena Cook for restoring me to spiritual health. Thanks to Dr. Howard Morgan, who awakened my love for the Jewish Roots of Christianity. Many thanks to Pastor Yesupadam, Founder of Love-N-Care Ministries, for your love and friendship. You are a true example of what a modern apostle should be. I'm eternally grateful to Dr. Michael Brown for allowing me the great privilege of sitting under his passionate teaching and preaching about Jesus during my initial training. Posthumous thanks to the late Wade E. Taylor, who's primary calling was the preparation of the Bride of Christ. Along with the others mentioned here, he is one of my great Christian heroes.

I also want to publicly acknowledge and appreciate the careful work and advice of my Editor, Sharon Whitby. Thanks Sharon. I'm certain that your grandfather, Wade Taylor, is pleased.

FOREWORD

S adly, **this book is not for everyone.** It's a highly concentrated, unfolding series of revelations concerning the Bride of Christ, that will be as dry as toast for all but the Sons of Almighty God.

> **Rom. 8:19** *"In fact, all creation is eagerly waiting for God to show who his children are."* CEV

In Christ, we are neither male nor female. Therefore, a man can be part of the Bride of Christ and a woman can be a Son of God. Only the Sons of God will understand and grow with the pages that follow. The Holy Spirit will add His living waters to this concentrated material, transforming it from dry powder into strong spiritual meat for the nourishment and edification of the Children of God. This book is in your hands, because it's time for you to arise.

The preparation of the Bride of Christ is my life message. I've studied, written and taught on it for over 20 years. I named this book *"The Wife of God"* to catch your eye. I knew that the title would be a bit provocative, so I subtitled it *"Fresh Revelation on the Bride of Christ"* to reveal the actual content. This is not intended to be a scholarly work, but I believe the theology is sound.

This book is not written from a Jewish perspective, because I'm not Jewish. I do try to present the Jewish understanding of many scriptures, but opinions vary. We will look at many Jewish wedding customs. Judaism spans approximately

4,000 years, and different things were done in different eras. In the first century, at the time of Jesus, there were Hellenistic Jews, Pharisees, Sadducees, Essenes and Zealots, with many variations in their customs. Today, there are Reform, Conservative, Orthodox and Ultra-Orthodox Jewish customs that differ from one another.

Opinions often strongly differ on what Jews believe and the customs they practice. My dear Jewish friend Dr. Howard Morgan once said, "*If you want three opinions, ask two Jews*." There is no central authority for Jewish Customs, and there are many variations on things that have been practiced over the years. I try to be accurate with the customs I explain, and I've footnoted the sources for customs I reference. Please remember that these things were done differently at different times by different groups. If you have a variation you'd like to share with me, please give me a source, and I'll consider corrections and/or revisions for future editions or Volume II.

Every verse in the Bible has at least five layers. In other words, you can read every scripture at least five different ways. First, every book was intended for a group of original recipients. For example, parts of Esther and Daniel were sent as circular flyers to the residents of the Persian Empire, and the book of Ephesians was first written to people living in first century Ephesus. The second layer, the Bible was intended for the Jewish People. Third, the books were intended to be applied to individual Jews. Fourth, every book can be applied to the Church. Fifth, the Scriptures are intended to be applied to us as individual Christians. Most new believers immediately jump to level five, but they could avoid a lot of problems by simply considering the other layers as well.

There is often another layer of Scripture that is prophetic or mystic. Not every verse in the Bible has this aspect, but many do. These are not all found exclusively in the traditional prophetic books. We will be looking at some verses concerning *The Wife of God* and *The Bride of Christ* from this mystic perspective. I will try to do justice to the traditional levels of understanding as well, but this book is uniquely intended as a revelatory look at the Bride of Christ.

TABLE OF CONTENTS

Endorsements v

Dedication and Thanks xi

Foreword xiii

Introduction xvii

Glossary of Hebraic Terms xxi

Abbreviations for Bible Versions xxiii

Chapter 1   The Wife of God 25

Chapter 2   The Bride of Christ 33

Chapter 3   Not Male or Female 40

Chapter 4   In the Beginning 45

Chapter 5   Rebekah the Willing Bride 51

Chapter 6   Ruth's Kinsman-Redeemer 57

Chapter 7   Esther and the Lion King 62

Chapter 8   Solomon's Song 70

Chapter 9   The Wedding at Mount Sinai .77

Chapter 10   The Wedding of the King's Son 84

Chapter 11   The Wedding at Cana 87

Chapter 12   John the Baptist 91

Chapter 13   The Dressing Room for Eternity 97

Chapter 14   The Bride Made Ready 105

Chapter 15   The Bride Price............................... 110

Chapter 16   The Last Supper 116

Chapter 17   Jesus Is Coming 122

Chapter 18   Consider Our Bridegroom 126

Chapter 19   Consider His Bride 134

Chapter 20   The Marriage Feast............................ 140

Chapter 21   The City of God 154

Addendum I: Hebraic Marriage Customs 161

Addendum II: The Seven Marriage Blessings 175

Suggested Reading..177

Bibliography.. 179

INTRODUCTION

The Living Parable

I believe the pages of this book contain an incredible **MYSTERY,** concerning your relationship with the Lord. In the Old Covenant, God often portrays Himself as the Husband and Israel as His Wife. In the New Covenant, Jesus is revealed as the Bridegroom and the Church as His intended Wife. *Marriage is an example of the covenant relationship He's extended to you.*

God uses comparative illustrations from earthly, human concepts to teach mankind about eternal things. We call these instructive comparisons *"parables."* The word *"parable"* comes from a Greek word that means "to place beside or compare."[1] Therefore, a parable is used to illustrate one subject by comparing it to another. In the Bible, these comparisons or short stories are used to teach hidden, spiritual truths.

Matrimony is a *"living parable,"* given by God, to teach us how to relate to Him. He uses this living parable all through the Bible to teach us about our relationship with the Lord. From our current position, bound in time, we can't observe the full details of our eternal union with Jesus, but Scripture reveals that we can have a deep, committed, personal relationship with Him that's *"like"* a good marriage.

---

[1] PC Study Bible, *Smith's Bible Dictionary* (CD-ROM, 2007), on "parables."

Paul wrote to the Ephesians describing a *"profound mystery"* that he says concerns *"Christ and the Church."* He quotes directly from Genesis, ***"For this reason a man will leave his father and mother and be united to his wife, and they will become one flesh."*** (Gen. 2:24 NIV) This is speaking about the union of Adam and Eve. The story is actual human history, recounting the creation of the first man and woman and their marital union, but Paul says their marriage somehow mysteriously points to Christ and the Church.

He implies that the Lord's intent is for Jesus to have a very close relationship with you, that's *similar* to a good marriage. He begins with some general household instruction and then delves into a unique revelation concerning our relationship with Christ. He quotes about Adam and Eve's union, and then says he's really talking about Christ and the Church. ***"'For this reason a man will leave his father and mother and be united to his wife, and the two will become one flesh.' This is a profound mystery — but I am talking about Christ and the church."*** (Eph. 5:31-32 NIV) This *living parable of marriage* is a multifaceted mystery that the entire Bible points toward. In the pages ahead we will unwrap this mystery.

Jesus wants to lovingly interact with each of us on a regular and continual basis. The Apostle Paul was not married, but he saw God's intentions for us to have a sacred relationship with the Lord that's similar to matrimony. Jesus was not married, but He spoke of it often, and He revealed Himself as our Bridegroom. As far as we know, the Apostle John never wed, but the Lord showed him the Marriage Supper of the Lamb and the Lamb's Wife as the City of New Jerusalem. Married or single, the *living parable of marriage* is sent from God as a descriptive love letter to you.

Jesus wants to share our lives, so that we might get to know each other as we experience life together. He looked on our earthly condition and saw that marriage is the most intimate, personal relationship that currently exists. He often uses stories about human love as parables to teach spiritual truth. Moving forward, I'll be sharing personal stories with you in an effort to illustrate key points.

Mary and I got married in 1981, and our relationship is a *"living parable."* We've spent endless hours together and shared a broad assortment of good times and bad. Together, we've dealt with sickness and the loss of loved ones. Together, we've celebrated the wonderful things of life that are common to all mankind. I knew Mary quite well when we were first married, but I certainly know her much better now. Our relationship has grown, because of our love and the time we've spent together. We've faced each day and shared whatever life has thrown at us over the years. The result is that we love each other more today than we did the day we were married. *That's the kind of ever deepening relationship Jesus wants to have with you.*

The Lord wants you to grow closer to Him as the years go by, just like a couple does in a good marriage. The Lord expects you to share life's good times and bad times with Him, just like a couple does. This is part of the **great mystery** Paul was trying to explain. In fact, what God wants to have with you and me is even deeper and more profound than what I've described. If you really want to know how close we can be to the Lord, you should look at a good marriage as our best example. Throughout the entire Bible, this mystery speaks of your current relationship and eternal future with Jesus.

God has hidden many things in His Word that can remain hidden, unless we prayerfully search them out. The Bible says, ***"It is the glory of God to conceal a thing: but the honor of kings is to search out a matter."*** (Prov. 25:2 KJV) As children of God, it is our honor to search out the deep things He has concealed. This mystery of marriage exemplifying our relationship with Christ, is one of those *"hidden"* things.

God is a Spirit and these are spiritual truths. As I began to write, the Lord spoke to my heart about *the Bride of Christ.* He said these truths have largely remained hidden, because most Christians don't yearn for a deeper relationship with Jesus. They read their Bibles, but don't have eyes to see what's written beneath the surface. We can only understand spiritual things if our spiritual eyes and ears are opened by the Holy Spirit. Friend, Jesus yearns for a deeper relationship with you. If you want more of Him, why don't we begin by praying about that together?

> *Dear Heavenly Father, I want to understand the living parable of marriage and how it relates to my relationship with Jesus. Please open my eyes to see what your Holy Spirit is saying. Lord, please use this book to draw me deeper in love with You. In Jesus' name, Amen.*

GLOSSARY OF HEBREW MARRIAGE TERMS

General Note: The following terms are taken from Hebrew, which has its own alphabet. These words are spelled out phonetically, but Hebrew pronunciations vary; therefore, the spelling of these words in English is subjective. [2]

ahavah: Love

arusah (arusot): Betrothed woman

bene huppah: Children of the huppah, or children of the bridechamber

be'rit: Covenant

be'rit nissuin: Marriage covenant

chatan: Groom

chuppah or huppah: The bridal canopy; as a legal term, the ceremony that completes the marriage

erusin: Betrothal, the first part of the marriage ceremony; not an engagement, technically, but in modern Hebrew *"erusin"* is "engagement"

ketubah or kethubah: Marriage contract

---

[2] This list has been modified slightly and I've made a few additions, but it is primarily drawn from Maurice Lamm's, *The Jewish Way in Love and Marriage* (Middle Village: Jonathan David, 1980), 276-283.

kiddushin: Sanctity; the betrothal stage of marriage that precedes *nussuin*; also used as a synonym for marriage

midrash: A genre of rabbinic literature extending from Talmudic times to the tenth century, which constitutes an anthology of homilies, and forms a running commentary to specific books of the Bible

mikveh or mikvah: A ritual pool used for purposes of ritual purification

Mishnah: Legal codification of Jewish law, redacted by Rabbi Judah ha-Nasi in the third century, on which the *Talmud* is based

mitzvah: Good deed, or commandment with religious overtones

mohar: A cash gift promised in the marriage contract by the groom to the bride. It is so important that it is called "the essence of the *ketubah*," or *ikkar ketubah*.

nussuin: Nuptials

shadkhan: Matchmaker

shidukhin: Conditions established upon an agreement to marry

Sheva Berakhot or Sheva Bachot: Seven marriage benedictions or blessings

shofar: A trumpet, traditionally made from a ram's horn

tallit or tallith: Prayer shawl

Talmud: The body of teaching that comprises the commentary and discussions of the Amoraim on the *Mishnah* of Rabbi Judah ha-Nasi. Its editing was completed c. 500 C.E.

tefillin: Phylacteries; black leather boxes bound to the arm and head during prayer

tevilah: Immersion in a *mikvah*

Torah: The five books of Moses; also used to encompass the concepts of Judaism

tze'niut: Modesty, privacy

yichud: Together; a couple alone in a room or enclosure; privacy; the term used to describe the Jewish concept of marital love; the ceremony that effects the second and final stage of the marriage ceremony

ABBREVIATIONS USED FOR DIFFERENT BIBLE VERSIONS

Unless otherwise noted by the following standard abbreviations, all scriptures used in this book are from the New International Version.

AMP	Amplified Bible
ASV	American Standard Version
BBE	Bible in Basic English
CEV	Contemporary English Version
CJB	Complete Jewish Bible
ESV	English Standard Version
GNT	Good News Translation
GOD'S WORD	God's Word Translation
KJV	King James Bible
NASB	New American Standard Bible
NCV	New Century Version
NKJV	New King James Bible
NIV	New International Bible
NIrV	New International Reader's Version
NLT	New Living Translation
NRSV	New Revised Standard Version

MSG	The Message
NET Bible	New English Translation
TEV	Today's English Version
TLB	The Living Bible
TNIV	Today's New International Version
RSV	Revised Standard Version
YLT	Young's Literal Translation

Chapter 1:

The Wife of God

W hen our youngest daughter was about two years old, she one day ran into our kitchen while I was making a pot of coffee. She playfully motioned me to stoop down to her level and I quickly complied. As I squatted on my heels, she took my face between her two small hands and looked deep into my eyes. While holding my face and my undivided attention she said, *"I just love you, so, so much."* With that, she laughingly released my face and ran out of the kitchen. Oddly, I was moved to tears as I was suddenly struck with the unexpected thought, *"I don't love God as much as my Rachael loves me, but I really want to."*

Somehow, the Holy Spirit had used my daughter's small demonstration of childlike love to move my heart in a way I'd never felt before. I was shocked as I realized that this simple demonstration of affection had exposed my own deep desire to love our unseen God. I wanted to know Him and love Him like my innocent child loved me. Then the questions arose, *"Does God want that as much as I do and is it even possible?"*

At the time, these thoughts were revolutionary for me, but I now know the Lord always intended His relationship with mankind to be loving and intimate. He often uses close human relationships as tools to teach us eternal truths about

Himself. In His Word, He calls Himself our Father and uses normal human relationships as examples to express His own love for us. God draws on the familiar, like a father and daughter, to teach us about His own deep feelings.

Beginning with Genesis and continuing throughout the Bible, the Lord reveals that He is seeking for those who desire to love Him and be with Him forever. His intentions toward us are like a good father, or an enamored suitor who hopes to marry an honorable wife. He speaks of Himself as our Husband or Bridegroom, and refers to mankind as His Wife or Bride. God has presented Himself as an eternal Bridegroom seeking an eternal Bride, so that we might know His heart toward us. Our God is the ultimate, eternal Lover. Love is not something God does, love is who He is. God is love and He looks for human beings who will return His love. *"I love those who love me, and those who seek me find me."* (Prov. 8:17 NIV)

In the Old Testament, the Lord often speaks of His marriage covenant promises to Israel. Many of the Biblical authors refer to the relationship between God and Israel in terminology that is normally reserved for marriage. Under the inspiration of the Holy Spirit, they used this language, even though they may not have fully understood that the Old Covenant was always intended to be a *Marriage Covenant*. The Lord has specific promises for Israel and the Jewish people, and for Christians, Israel is also a type of the Bride of Christ. The Old Covenant is a *Marriage* Covenant that was given to Israel, and it is the foreshadowing of the New *Marriage* Covenant that's revealed in the New Testament, extended to the rest of mankind.

The book of Genesis tells us that God created both male and female human beings *"in the image of God."* (Gen. 1:27) The Creation narrative in Genesis 1 demonstrates that the Lord affirmed the goodness of His new creations at the end of each cycle by proclaiming *"it is good."* At the creation of man, the Lord observed a higher level of satisfaction by saying that man was *"very good."* The first time the Lord ever said *"it is not good"* was when He saw that Adam was lonely. *"And the Lord God said, It is not good that the man should be alone."* (Gen. 2:18 NKJV) Since we are created in the image of God, the Lord may have been expressing His own desire for companionship and love when He declared *"it is not good that the man should be alone."* Perhaps He was really saying, *"It is not good for **Me** to be alone."* This may be an early prophetic look at the Lord's plan to take a Bride for Himself from among the children of men.[3]

Abraham was the first Hebrew and the father of faith. Christians sometimes point to the marriage of his son Isaac to Rebekah as a type of the relationship between Jesus and the Church. In this analogy, Isaac's father Abraham is representative of God the Father; Isaac is symbolic of Jesus; Rebekah is representative of the Bride of Christ; and the unnamed servant of Abraham who sought out Rebekah as Isaac's bride, is symbolic of the Holy Spirit. In this prophetic foreshadowing, Rebekah the Gentile marries Isaac, the first natural-born Jew. Additionally, this was the first Jewish wedding and it contains the seeds of many marriage customs that have been carried down in Jewish weddings for the last 3,500 years. (Gen. 24:1-67)

In Exodus, the Lord initiated a covenant with the nation of Israel through Moses at Mount Sinai. Many rabbis have taught that this was actually a marriage covenant between the Lord and Israel. A well-known Messianic Jewish writer from the last century said, *"Moses brought forth the people out of the camp to meet with God; while Jehovah, as the bridegroom, meets His Church at Sinai."*[4] The modern Jewish scholar Ronald L. Eisenberg said, *"For the Rabbis, marriage symbolized other perfect relationships, such as those between God and Israel."*[5] Rabbinic

---

[3] S.J. Hill, *Burning Desire* (Orlando: Relevant Books, 2005), 3.

[4] Alfred Edersheim, *Sketches of Jewish Social Life in the Days of Christ* (London: The Religious Track Society, 1908), 153.

[5] Ronald L. Eisenberg, *The JPS Guide to Jewish Traditions* (Philadelphia: The Jewish Publication Society, 2004), 31.

sages have long understood that the Old Covenant is not a Jewish law book; it is a *Marriage Covenant*.

In Deuteronomy, we find the following verse: ***"Love the Lord your God with all your heart and with all your soul and with all your strength."*** (Deut. 6:5 NIV) Moses wrote this verse under the infallible inspiration of the Holy Spirit. Later, when Jesus is asked what He believes to be the most important thing in the Bible, He quotes the above verse from Deuteronomy and affirms that to love God is the most important thing in the Bible.[6] In other words, Jesus said that the commandment for mankind to *"love the Lord"* is the very purpose for our existence and the first thing we need to understand. It's quite significant that loving Him is the most important thing in the Bible and the objective of our lives. This invitation to *"love"* God was first offered to Israel, and it speaks to us of the Covenant He has graciously extended to His people. It's *"like"* a good marriage.

There are many important marriages in the Bible that teach lessons about God's love for us. Four entire books of the Old Testament present the parable of God's marriage to Israel in the context of human courtship and marriage: Ruth, Esther, Song of Solomon and Hosea. These were all real marriages involving real people, but they teach us about our relationship with the Lord. As previously mentioned, for the rabbis, marriage often symbolized the relationship between God and Israel. Of course, the representative meanings of these marriage relationships are often viewed differently by Jews and Christians, but both agree that they express aspects of God's love for mankind.

In the book of Ruth, a poor young woman marries a wealthy older man. The relationship between Boaz and Ruth is representational of God's loving relationship with Israel, with Boaz representing the Lord and Ruth representing Israel.

---

6 Mark 12:28b *"Of all the commandments, which is the most important?"* 29 *"The most important one,"* answered Jesus, *"is this: 'Hear, O Israel, the Lord our God, the Lord is one. 30 Love the Lord your God with all your heart and with all your soul and with all your mind and with all your strength.'"* NIV

For Christians, Boaz the Jew can also be looked on as a type of Christ, and Ruth the Gentile can be viewed as a type of the Bride of Christ. Ruth marries Boaz as her kinsman-redeemer and ultimately becomes the mother of Obed, whom Matthew's Gospel tells us was the ancestor of Joseph, the human father of Jesus.

The foreshadowing of the Bride of Christ can also be found in the book of Esther, where once again a poor girl marries a wealthy older man. King Ahasuerus/Xerxes is a type of Christ. The King's first wife, Vashti, is a type of unfaithful Israel, who refused to come to her King when she was called. Esther herself is a type of the Bride of Christ. The murderous villain known as Haman, is a type of Satan. Esther's cousin Mordecai and the king's servant Hegai direct Esther in her bridal preparation, demonstrating functions that are typical of the Holy Spirit. In this story, Ahasuerus is a Gentile and Esther is a Jew. Together, they overcome the plans of wicked Haman/Satan and live happily ever after.

The Song of Solomon has traditionally been understood to be an allegory of human romantic love that also speaks about the Lord's relationship with Israel. For Christians, the book also speaks about the relationship between Christ and His Church. We hold that King Solomon, as the son of David, is a type of Jesus and the Shulamite is a type of the redeemed individual and the entire Bride of Christ. One Christian source comments, "*There is a beautiful interchange of character, name, and blessedness between the heavenly Solomon and His Shulamite, the redeemed church.*"[7] Song of Solomon speaks first about the relationship between the Lord and Israel, and secondarily about the Lord Jesus and the Church/Bride of Christ.

Most of the book of Hosea is written as an allegory of the Lord's relationship with Israel. In the first chapter, Hosea is instructed to take a prostitute named Gomer for his wife. The book explains that Gomer is symbolic of unfaithful Israel, and faithful Hosea represents the Lord. The reader is made to understand

---

[7] PC Study Bible, *Fausset's Bible Dictionary* (CD-ROM, 2007), on "Shulamite."

that this is how the Lord sees His relationship with ancient Israel; with God steadfast in His committed love and Israel often running off to worship other gods, as a prostitute with other lovers. It also contains the redemptive promises of marriage from God to the Jewish people, recited daily by observant Jews. Christians need to consider the message of Hosea and understand that, like the Jewish people before us, we often are unfaithful in our devotion toward Him, but He is always faithful toward us.

For Christians, these Old Testament marriages can be looked on as prophetic foreshadowings of what God intends for His Son Jesus and His Bride, the Church. We will look at some of these marriages in more depth later and discuss their typology for the Bride of Christ. The reader should note that most of these unions are between Jews and Gentiles, symbolizing the engrafting of the Gentiles into the spiritual family of Israel. (Rom. 11) **The Church should always remember that God has not replaced the Jewish people with Christians, but rather, we have been joined into their spiritual family by our faith in the one true God of Israel.**

God explicitly declares Himself to be Israel's Husband in several other places in the Prophets. Isaiah penned, *"For your Maker is your husband — the LORD Almighty is his name — the Holy One of Israel is your Redeemer; he is called the God of all the earth."* (Isa. 54:5 NIV) And he wrote, "As a young man marries a maiden, so will your sons marry you; as a **bridegroom** *rejoices over* **his bride,** *so will* **your God** *rejoice over you."* (Isa. 62:5 NIV) Jeremiah also points to the Lord as Israel's Husband, *"Return, faithless people,"* declares the LORD, *"for* **I am your husband."** (Jer. 3:14 NIV) And he identifies Israel as God's Bride, *"I remember the devotion of your youth, how as a* **bride you loved me** *and followed me through the desert, through a land not sown."* (Jer. 2:2b NIV) **The Prophets speak often of Israel as God's Bride and the Lord as Israel's Bridegroom.** This tender language is meant to give Israel, and the Church by extension, a clear perspective on how the Lord views His intended relationship with them.

Continuing with the idea of Israel as the Lord's Bride or Wife, the Prophets refer to Israel's sin of idolatry as whoredom and adultery committed against their spiritual Husband. *"They committed adultery with their idols."* (Ezek. 23:37b NIV) *"'But you have lived as a prostitute with many lovers...' declares the LORD."* (Jer. 3:1b NIV) *"I have seen thine adulteries, and thy neighings, the lewdness of thy whoredom."* (Jer. 13:27 KJV) *"The land is guilty of the vilest adultery in departing from the LORD."* (Hos. 1:2 NIV) *"'But like a woman unfaithful to her husband, so you have been unfaithful to me, O house of Israel,' declares the LORD."* (Jer. 3:20 NIV) The Bible repeatedly compares the Lord's emotional pain caused by Israel's unfaithful behavior to a married person's feelings when his/her spouse is discovered to be sexually unfaithful.

In August of 2011, I was in India for a short writing sabbatical. I spent a lot of time specifically pondering the love stories that reveal the heart of God in the Bible. I woke in the middle of the night, repeating over and over again in my heart, *"I want to know You as much as You can be known."* As I prayed, my daughter Rachael, who is now a young woman, was sleeping in the room next to mine. I remembered her as my precious little girl holding my face in the kitchen all those years ago, while looking deep into my eyes and expressing her child-like love for me. I remembered my heart's cry to have that kind of love for God.

I remembered Moses, the great lover of God, who we sometimes call *"the Lawgiver."* This man loved God as few ever have, and he was allowed to know Him so well that the Bible says he knew Him, *"face to face."* (Ex. 33:11) Moses was a man captivated by God's love, and somehow, God allowed him to know Him *"face to face."* I want to hold the face of Jesus and look into His eyes. I want to tell the Lord, *"I just love You, so, so much."* My innermost being cries out for that type of interaction with God.

Please allow me to share another brief story, that will resonate only with the people to whom this book is actually written. Jesus came and stood next to my bed one morning as I lay in the state between waking and sleeping. I sensed His manifest presence, but didn't open my eyes. Words are inadequate to describe what this felt like.

He leaned over me and put His face next to mine, as if to whisper a secret in my ear, but He didn't speak. Silently, His face touched the surface of my face, instantly electrifying my entire body. As I'm writing about this now, every hair on my body is again standing up, as if I'm in an electric field.

Suspended in time, we were face to face. Then, His face moved into my face, no longer constrained by the surface of my skin. His love welcomed me and seemed to say this type of interaction was His constant desire for those who long for Him. My inner man experienced an instant shift from the temporal realm into the eternal. I moved into a place of His presence that I had not known existed.

I think I was conscious, but perhaps I was still asleep? When He disengaged and withdrew, I opened my eyes. The entire episode transpired in less than sixty seconds, but I knew this taste of eternity would be with me for the rest of my life. As I wondered at the reality of what I had just sensed, I struggled to know if it was a dream or a real visitation. My answer came the next morning, when He came to me again in the same way...

Friends, the Bible teaches that such intimacy is possible. **This is eternity's greatest love story.** You were born for intimacy with God. If you want to know Jesus face to face, you must desire Him more than life itself. He alone must become your all-consuming passion. **He's the only answer for your family, the Jewish people and the entire Church.**

As we conclude this chapter, I want to pray for you with words that are drawn from the Song of Solomon. *"May the Holy Spirit draw you and place you as a seal over the heart of God. May your love for Him be as strong as death. May He cause your love to burn like a blazing fire and a mighty flame of passion. May nothing, including the grave, separate you from the Ancient of Days. In Jesus' name."*

CHAPTER 2:

The Bride of Christ

Matt. 22:1 *"AND AGAIN **Jesus spoke** to them in parables* (comparisons, stories used to illustrate and explain), *saying, 2 **The kingdom of heaven is like a king who gave a wedding banquet for his son.***"* AMP

In the middle 1990s I volunteered for an organization that served children who had cancer. We held an annual golf tournament-fundraiser that featured Jim Kelly, a future Hall of Fame quarterback who started in four Super Bowls. He was well known and had quite a following in the 1990s and still does. He'd lend us his name and donate time to help us draw big crowds, raising much needed awareness and support to benefit the children. He was always very personal with the kids and their families, and though I didn't know him well, I really appreciated and admired him for his generosity and kindness.

One day, we were both in my car driving to an autograph signing event. It was early in the morning, and he asked me to stop for some sausage biscuits and coffee. As we were sitting in the drive-through line, I was thinking about all the people who had paid money to see him and get his autograph. I was amused that he was sitting in my car at Burger King, while hundreds of people were waiting in line at our fundraiser to see him.

I really appreciated Jim's work with our organization, but I was fairly ignorant of his football statistics and achievements. We were having a pleasant visit over a fast food breakfast, while driving to an event packed with fans that knew more about his public history and sports exploits than I did. Daydreaming, while driving and eating my biscuit, I had this thought, *"If any of those "fans" ever actually showed up at his house, he wouldn't know them and he might call the police, but if I showed up he'd probably invite me to come in."* It struck me as being ironic that his *"fans,"* thousands or perhaps even millions of them, knew more *about* him than I did, but I actually knew him and they didn't. **These things made me think about how people relate to Jesus.**

As that day unfolded, the Lord began to speak to me about fans versus friends. He showed me that like sports heroes, Jesus has many fans who know lots of things about Him, but He has few friends who actually know Him. Sticking with my analogy, the New Testament teaches that if a "fan" showed up at Heaven's front door and asked to come in because he knew all the stories about Jesus, sadly he would be rejected. But, if someone who actually knows Christ shows up at the Father's house, the Bible says he'll be welcomed in, not as a fan, and not as a friend, but as part of the Lord's Bridal Company.

The New Testament clearly reveals that Jesus wants people to know Him and become part of His family. The Lord is not looking for fans. He wants intimate, loving relationships with people He can know and relate to, like they would in a good marriage. I was raised in the Church, but I didn't become a born-again believer until I was fifteen years old. Like many, I had been attending church as a fan of Jesus, but the Bible teaches that until I established a personal relationship with Him, I was still lost. (John 3:15-18) Being a church-attending fan was not enough. I didn't comprehend that Jesus could really be known and I certainly had no understanding that He desired to know me as my spiritual *"**Bridegroom**."*

Jesus is the Messiah. The word *Messiah* comes from a Hebrew word that means *"anointed one."* This same word in the New Testament is translated from Greek as *Christ*. **In the Old Testament, the concept of the Messiah as the Bridegroom and the Church as the Bride is hidden in types and foreshadowing images of God as Husband and Israel as His Wife.** In the New Testament, this is still a mystery, but it's more clearly developed and revealed. The term *"Bride of Christ"* is not used in Scripture, but the concept of the Church being the intended Wife of Jesus is quite well-developed, and **the New Testament gives us a progressively deeper revelation of Jesus as the Messiah/ Bridegroom and the Church as the intended Bride of Christ.**

Jesus often alluded to Himself as the **Bridegroom.** *"Jesus answered, 'How can **the guests of the bridegroom** mourn while he is with them? The time will come when the **bridegroom** will be taken from them; then they will fast.'"* (Matt. 9:15 NIV) This same direct quote from Jesus was also recorded in Mark 2:19-20 and Luke 5:34-35. By presenting Himself as the Bridegroom, Jesus was building on the prophetic foreshadowing contained in the Old Testament, of a marriage between God and His people. He was also declaring that He is the fulfillment of the promises for Israel's Messiah.

John the Baptist was asked if he was the Messiah. He clearly said he was not. He then identified Jesus as the Bridegroom and those who followed Him as His Bride. *"You yourselves can testify that I said, '**I am not the Messiah** but am sent ahead of him.' **The bride belongs to the bridegroom.** The friend who attends the **bridegroom** waits and listens for him, and is full of joy when he hears the **bridegroom's** voice. That joy is mine, and it is now complete."* (John 3:28-29 NIV)

Paul also identified Jesus as the Bridegroom and His followers as His Bride. He wrote to the Corinthian church and told them that when he led them into a relationship with Jesus, he was really bringing them into a betrothal. He spoke in unveiled terms of Christ as the Husband and the Church as a virgin promised to Him in marriage. *"I am jealous for you with a godly jealousy. **I promised you to**

one husband, to Christ, so that I might present you as a pure virgin to him." (2 Cor. 11:2 NIV) Paul identified Jesus as the Bridegroom and likened himself to a father who had arranged a marriage by introducing the people to Jesus.

Paul taught believers that they had been joined to the Lord in a relationship that should be compared to marriage. When dealing with the issue of immorality among believers, he cautioned them that they were being unfaithful to the Lord by committing sexual sins. He taught this principle by alluding to the foundation of Adam and Eve's union in Genesis 2:24. He wrote these words to the Corinthian Church and to each of us, *"Do you not know that he who unites himself with a prostitute is one with her in body? For it is said, 'The two will become one flesh.' But whoever is united with the Lord is one with him in spirit."* (1 Cor. 6:16-17 NIV) His point is that in a mystic sense, believers who commit sexual sins are being spiritually joined to others and thus, they are committing infidelity against their Husband, Jesus.

The New Testament gives us many parables, teachings and stories set in the context of weddings to bring us a deeper revelation of the Bride of Christ. The story of *"The Wedding at Cana,"* where Jesus turned water into wine, is contained in the Gospel of John. (John 2:1-11) This wedding is the setting for the first public appearance and the first miracle of Jesus the Messiah; *"This, the first of his signs."* (John 2:11 ESV) This first presentation of power in the context of a wedding, points to Jesus' eternal ministry purpose being related to His ultimate wedding with the Church.

Jesus used parables to teach us about the Bride of Christ and about His plans. We find one of the clearest examples of "Bride of Christ" wedding imagery in the twenty-second chapter of Matthew's Gospel. *"AND AGAIN Jesus spoke to them in parables (comparisons, stories used to illustrate and explain), saying, The kingdom of heaven is like a king who gave a wedding banquet for his son."* (Matt. 22:1-2 AMP) Jesus begins the story with this amazing statement, *"The kingdom of heaven is like a king who gave a wedding banquet for his son."* The *"king"* speaks of God the Father. *"His son"* speaks of Jesus Christ. The *"wedding"* speaks of the relationship you were created to have with God. Clearly, what follows is about the Lord's Kingdom, and it's compared to a wedding. Jesus was declaring Himself to be the King's Son and our Messiah. The pending **marriage of the King's Son** is central to the entire story. The Old Testament marriage of the Lord to Israel would have been familiar to the original Jewish hearers of Jesus' story, and the connection He was trying to make would have been confusing or terribly offensive to those who did not receive Him as Messiah and Son of God.

In Matthew, Jesus also gives us *"The Parable of the Wise and Foolish Virgins,"* contained in chapter twenty-five. This chapter and the one that precedes it are speaking of the timing of the return of Jesus Christ to earth. He introduces Himself into the story when He refers to *"the Bridegroom"* in the following, *"At that time the kingdom of heaven will be like ten virgins who took their lamps and went out to meet **the bridegroom**."* (Matt. 25:1 NIV) This parable again gives us the setting of a wedding to teach us about the return of Jesus and the fulfillment of the Kingdom of Heaven.

No look at the Bride of Christ in the New Testament would be complete without including the prophetic visions of the **Apostle John** in *Revelation*. He looked down through eternity and saw the Bride of Christ fully prepared for her Husband. He penned these words that are the clearest reference in the New Testament to the Marriage of Jesus Christ to His Bride, *"Let us rejoice and be glad and give him glory!* **For the wedding of the Lamb has come,** *and **his bride has made herself ready**."* (Rev. 19:7 NIV) The New Testament reveals that Jesus is the Lamb of God, who takes away the sin of the world. (John 1:29) The *"wedding of the Lamb"* is clearly, **the Wedding of Jesus Christ.** The true Church is *"his bride"* who *"has made herself ready,"* indicating a **corporate** responsibility on the Bride's part to be *"ready"* for our wedding day. Salvation is a free gift, but we must **collectively** submit to the principles of Scripture to become the Bride who has made herself ready.

John also spoke of those who would be invited to a wedding supper to celebrate this union between Christ and His Church. *"Then the angel said to me, 'Write: "Blessed are those who are invited to **the wedding supper of the Lamb!**"'* And he added, 'These are the true words of God.'* (Rev. 19:9 NIV) This reminds us of the words of Jesus, *"The kingdom of heaven is like a king who gave **a wedding banquet for his son."*** (Matt. 22:2 AMP) John saw that time as we know it would end and eternity would begin with Christ and His Bride together, at the *"wedding supper of the Lamb."*

John went on to speak of a vast Bridal Company that would live with the Lord in the city of New Jerusalem. He spoke of the occupants of that city being prepared corporately as a Bride for Jesus, her Husband. *"And I John saw the holy city, new Jerusalem, coming down from God out of heaven, **prepared as a bride adorned for her husband."*** (Rev. 21:2 KJV) He said the Lord would actually dwell there with His Bride. Using the consistent New Testament theme of Jesus as the Lamb of God, the Angel of the Lord told John, *"I will show you the bride, the Lamb's wife."* (Rev. 21:9 NKJV) He identified this *"Bride/Lamb's Wife"* as the occupants of the *"holy city of New Jerusalem."*

The Lord showed John that our former Earthly reality will pass away. The Bride of Christ will be joined to the Lord and live with Him in the City of New Jerusalem as we move into eternity. (Rev. 21:3-10) He concludes his majestic book in the very last chapter of the Bible with the Bride of Christ working together with the Holy Spirit to invite others to join the eternal Bridal Company while time still remains. *"The **Spirit and the bride** say, 'Come!' And let him who hears say, 'Come!' Whoever is thirsty, let him come; and whoever wishes, let him take the free gift of the water of life."* (Rev. 22:17 NIV)

As we see the culmination of our time on earth coming down to a Wedding and a Bride, I'm reminded of my story about the pro-football quarterback, concerning fans versus friends. Fans know facts and figures about someone, but friends actually know the person. Married people move far beyond friendship into an exclusive, lifetime commitment. This committed relationship is built on love that grows stronger with the years.

Sadly, most Christians are not much more than fans of Jesus Christ. They know things about Him, but don't really know Him. Some "Christians" met Jesus years ago and have never spoken to Him since. In a good marriage, you spend time with your spouse and grow closer to them as the years go by. You don't meet them one time and call it a great marriage. Even if you continue to see someone for a quick "*intimate*" meeting once a week, we still call that an affair and not a marriage. Churches are full of spiritual affairs, where someone meets with the Lord once or twice a week in a service, and then goes on with the rest of their life as if He doesn't exist. **Jesus is not looking for fans, and He doesn't want affairs.**

Jesus wants for you to relate to Him in love, like a good marriage. Perhaps you've relegated your interaction with the Lord to church meetings or prayers before meals? The Lord put this book into your hands in an effort to draw you deeper, and you're reading it because you desire the same. Jesus loves you and wants to be with you always. **You've been called and chosen by God to become part of the Bride of Christ. Purpose in your heart that you'll allow Jesus continuous full access to your everyday life and you'll not relegate Him to anything less. This is the eternal plan of the ages for you.**

CHAPTER 3:

Not Male or Female

When I was about ten years old, my mother gave me a book entitled *"For Boys Only."* I understood from Mom's nervous instructions that this book was supposed to explain my still developing sexuality and define my future role as a man. After taking the book to my room, I looked to see if there were any pictures, and finding none, I quickly lost interest and never actually read it. Even though I didn't read the book, everything worked out well for me. I've always loved being a guy, and I never really struggled with any "gender issues" until I found out that God wanted me to be His Bride! For guys, it can be real threatening to try to see yourself as a "Bride."

When I came into the Kingdom of God as a young teenager, I discovered that the Bible says, *"there is neither... male nor female... in Christ Jesus."* (Gal. 3:28 NIV) I didn't understand that, because I was definitely still seeing BIG differences between males and females. Before I could begin to decipher that mysterious truth, I was also informed that Christian girls were called to become *"sons of God"* and Christian guys were supposed to become *"The Bride of Christ."* These were difficult concepts for a happy, fairly well-adjusted, fifteen-year-old male. My dilemma was not unique.

The Bible is the infallible Word of God, but the chapter divisions are the imperfect work of men. Galatians 3:28-4:7 continues the same subject and should not be divided. Paul says *there is neither male nor female in Christ Jesus,* then goes on to explain that males and females in Christ can both become *sons of God* and joint heirs of His Kingdom.[8] The Lord God is a Spirit (John 4:24), and our inner being is spirit. When we pass from this life, we will remain who we've become in Christ, but we don't go with our human private parts. We're created in the image of God; not in body, but in spirit. Our spirits are neither male nor female, Jew nor Greek. This means that sexual and racial distinctions are reserved for the days of our flesh. (Matt. 22:30) Here the distinctions are real, but in eternity we'll be transformed into immortal beings that are like our God. (1 John 3:2) Understanding this concept and knowing that God uses things from our human experience to teach us about eternity, long ago helped me embrace my role in the **Bride of Christ**.

Dr. Michael Brown enlightened me further by pointing out the following:

> *What's important to understand about the bridal paradigm is that **it's never individual; it's always corporate**. In other words, **just as an individual Jew did not see himself in any feminized way as part of a Bride**, in the same way **individual Christians are not to see themselves as somehow part of a Bride in relation to Jesus in a personal way**, other than to relate to Him as Lord, Master, Savior; whether they are male or female.*[9]

---

[8] Gal 3:28 **There is neither** *Jew nor Greek, slave nor free,* **male nor female,** *for you are all one in Christ Jesus.... Gal 4:6 Because* **you are sons,** *God sent the Spirit of his Son into our hearts, the Spirit who calls out, "Abba, Father." 7 So you are no longer a slave, but* **a son; and since you are a son, God has made you also an heir.** NIV

[9] Michael L. Brown, *Personal Interview*, September 6, 2008.

The Jewish people understood that *collectively,* they were called to be **God's Wife** at Mount Sinai. Christian men and women are called to be part of a "*corporate*" **Bridal Company.** We will never be individual guys in wedding dresses, walking the aisle with Jesus. The Bride of Christ is not a male/female thing, but rather a human concept that God has presented to explain His loving and honorable intentions toward us. *"There is neither... male nor female, for you are all one in Christ Jesus...Because you are his sons."* (Gal. 3:28, 4:6 NIV) We must understand that God speaks to us in our humanity, and He uses human concepts to explain sacred truth beyond our mortal experience.

In the Kingdom of God there is neither male nor female, so a woman can be a *"son"* and a guy can be a *"bride."* In western Christianity we have spent so much time focused on getting people to have a personal relationship with Jesus, that we've sometimes neglected the idea of a corporate relationship with the Lord. Paul wrote, *"in Christ we, though many, form one body, and each member belongs to all the others."* (Rom. 12:5 NIV) This means that just as we have an individual relationship with the Lord that is exclusively our own, we also have a corporate relationship with the Lord that is shared with all other believers. It also means that we have a shared responsibility for our corporate growth with other believers. Jesus prayed that we would embrace this distinctive unity, *"My prayer is...that all of them may be one."* (John 17:20-21 NIV) **The Bride of Christ is a communal identity that we must embrace to become one in Christ.**

Look at the Bride in Revelation, where she is portrayed as the collective residents of the city of New Jerusalem. *"I saw the **Holy City, the new Jerusalem,** coming down out of heaven from God, prepared as a **bride** beautifully dressed for her **husband.**"* (Rev. 21:2 NIV) Alluding to the Bride of Christ, John tells us that the city of New Jerusalem is prepared as a *"bride,"* and *"her husband"* is Jesus. In even clearer language, John goes on to write, *"One of the seven angels...said to me, 'Come, I will show you **the bride, the wife of the Lamb.'** And he...showed me **the Holy City, Jerusalem,** coming down out of heaven from God."* (Rev. 21:9-10

NIV) *"The bride,"* also known as the *"wife of the Lamb,"* is comprised of the occupants of the Holy City, Jerusalem. **The Bride is made up of the redeemed saints from all time, living together as a communal Bride with Jesus in the holy City of New Jerusalem.**

Godly men and women need to embrace the concept of being part of a Bridal Company. There will be an event called the Marriage of the Lamb (Rev. 19:7) and all the redeemed of the ages will be there, but this is spiritual language conveying spiritual truth. We will be one Bridal Company, no longer divided by the ethnic and physical attributes that often influence our lives on earth. When we stand before God on that great day, there will be neither male nor female, Jew nor Greek. There will only be those who have committed their lives to serving Jesus and being prepared for the Marriage of the ages.

Many women have an easy time relating to the Lord as a Bride. When I've shared this collective character of the Bride, some ladies have gotten offended with me. I think they were upset because they had no problem seeing themselves standing in a celestial wedding dress next to the risen carpenter from Galilee, but they couldn't visualize the group photo with all the other believers at the same wedding. Ladies, don't shoot the messenger here. If you doubt my take on this, keep reading. Search the Scriptures for yourselves. (Acts 17:11)

I think it's easier for guys to relate to a Bridal Company than it is to see themselves individually as a bride; and truly that assembly idea is the correct picture. We live in an age of gender confusion, but these truths transcend human anatomy. God created you to be the person you are, and, male or female, He wants to relate to you as part of His Bridal Company. **The Bride of Christ is a group identity; it is not a personal thing.** The Bride of Christ is not male or female. It's a Bridal Company of saints with no distinction made for ethnic identity or physical gender.

Friends, whoever you are, Jesus loves you and wants to know you. You need to recognize that the Creator of the Universe is inviting you into an eternal union with Himself. What He's offering is beyond our human experience. If you want to get a glimpse at what's intended, **come along** as we study this amazing mystery. **There is one God and Savior and He will have one united** *"Bride,"* **not many individual** *"brides."* Your place in the Bride is uniquely your own. Without you, the Bride will be incomplete. **The Holy Spirit and the Bride say,** *"come."* [10]

---

[10] Rev. 22:17 *The Spirit and the bride say,* **"Come!"** *And let him who hears say,* **"Come!"** *Whoever is thirsty, let him* **come;** *and whoever wishes, let him take the free gift of the water of life.* NIV

CHAPTER 4:

In the Beginning

⚜

First meetings and first opinions are very important. I was playing ping-pong the first time I ever saw my future wife. We were both students at the University of South Carolina. I loved to play Table Tennis in the Student Union whenever I had a little spare time, so that's where she found me. Mary challenged the table, and when her turn came, we introduced ourselves over the game. Her skill level was not very high, but she looked really good and I loved her voice. I asked her out and we started seeing each other soon after. That's where our relationship first began, and it ultimately led to our marriage. She still looks good to me and I still love her voice.

When you want to study a particular scriptural subject in depth, you should begin by seeing where it's first mentioned in the Bible. This well-known principle is known as *"The Law of First Mention."* Of course, Genesis is the first book of the Bible, and as such, it contains many *first-mentions*. Adam and Eve are **the first man and woman.** Genesis recounts their creation and mankind's **first marital union, with God bringing them together.** For Christians and Jews, earth's **first marriage** became a Biblical template for many wedding practices. **This union also speaks to us prophetically about the relationship between Jesus and His Bride, in many significant ways.**

Jewish weddings historically feature **a seven-day celebration that represents the seven days of creation.** Jacob celebrated with his brides, Leah and Rachel, for seven days.[11] At his own wedding, Samson put forward a riddle that had to be answered *"within the seven days of the feast."*[12] To this day, a **seven-day celebration feast** is still practiced by some Jewish sects. For Christians, the extended wedding feast speaks of the Marriage Supper of the Lamb.[13] It also speaks to us of eternity celebrated with Jesus. The wedding represents a new creation and a new world.[14]

There are seven blessings spoken at many Jewish weddings. They are known as ***Sheva Bachot*** which means *"Seven Blessings"* in Hebrew. These *Seven Blessings* trace their origins to the distant past, including the marriage of Adam and Eve. In addition to the seven days of creation, some think this practice is based on the Lord's first blessing over mankind in Genesis 1:28; God blessed with seven specific themes mentioned. *"**God blessed** them and said to them, 'Be fruitful and increase in number; fill the earth and subdue it. Rule over the fish of the sea and the birds of the air and over every living creature that moves on the ground.'"* Many Jews see the Bible's first commandment, *"**Be fruitful and increase in number,**"* as meaning *"**have lots of babies.**"*

Pointing to Creation and the sevenfold blessing of Adam and Eve, there is a very specific connection to Eden in the sixth blessing of the *Sheva Bachot.*

---

[11] Gen. 29:27 *"Finish this daughter's **bridal week**; then we will give you the younger one also, in return for another seven years of work." 28 And Jacob did so. He finished **the week** with Leah, and then Laban gave him his daughter Rachel to be his wife.* NIV

[12] Judges 14:10 *And there Samson held **a feast, as was customary for young men.** 11 When the people saw him, they chose thirty men to be his companions. 12 "Let me tell you a riddle," Samson said to them. "If you can give me the answer within the **seven days of the feast,** I will give you thirty linen garments and thirty sets of clothes."* NIV

[13] Rev. 19:9 "Write this: Blessed are those who are invited to the wedding supper of the Lamb!" NIV

[14] Rabbi Aryeh Kaplan, *Made in Heaven* (New York: Moznaim Publishing, 1983), 178.

*O make these beloved companions greatly rejoice even as Thou didst rejoice in **Thy creation in the Garden of Eden as of old**. Blessed art Thou, O Lord, who makest bridegroom and bride to rejoice.* [15]

After the ceremony itself, the presiding clergy lifts a cup of wine known as *"the cup of blessing,"* as he recites each of the seven formal blessings.[16] Perhaps Paul was alluding to this marriage custom when he spoke about Holy Communion, saying, *"**The cup of blessing** which we bless, is it not the communion of the blood of Christ?"*[17] Again, with an eye toward Creation, some believe that God Himself took *the cup of blessing* and spoke the marriage blessings over Adam and Eve in the Garden of Eden as Michael and Gabriel stood by acting as the **Children of the Bride Chamber** or **Friends of the Bridegroom**.[18]

Adam and Eve were the first couple to have a relationship with God. In other words, *in the beginning*, they experienced Him together. This is another very important first principle that comes from their marriage. Because God plays a key role in the Jewish home, marriage is represented by a triangle involving three parties: the husband, the wife, and God.[19] I think the *triangle* is a perfect analogy, with man and woman related to each other horizontally on the bottom and connected vertically with God at the top. I believe this is the pattern for our Churches, with sanctified people at the bottom and Jesus at the top.

---

[15] Quoted from Addendum II.

[16] Howard Morlock, *Jewish Faith and the New Covenant* (Nan Nuys: Rock of Israel, 1980), 107.

[17] 1 Cor. 10:16 KJV.

[18] Edersheim, *Sketches,* 154.

[19] Wilfred R. Kent, *The Greatest Love Story...Ever Told* (Pretoria: TWM International, 1995), 124-125.

God created man in His own image, and their marriage was the pinnacle of Creation; so every marriage points back to the Lord's original plans for mankind.[20] The bride and groom are considered sinless at their wedding ceremony, in part, because Adam and Eve were married before they sinned.[21] Bridal garments are normally made of white linen, which represents holiness and forgiveness. These white garments also signify that the bride and groom are considered sinless on their wedding day.[22]

Adam and Eve had this type of shared relationship with the Lord before they sinned. From a Christian perspective, God's desire is that we would once again relate to Him in innocence. We can be free from our sins because of what Jesus has done for us at the Cross. Without spot or blemish, we can relate to each other as members of the Bride, and together we can relate to Jesus as our Bridegroom. This corporate aspect of *"the Church"* as the spotless Bride of Christ is largely missing, but by God's grace it will come.

When talking about the relationship between husbands and wives, Paul quotes from Genesis 2:24 in Ephesians 5:31, *"For this reason a man will leave his father and mother and be united to his wife, and **the two will become one flesh**."* He explains in the next verse that Adam and Eve's marriage is supposed to teach us about Jesus and the Church. ***"This is a profound mystery — but I am talking about Christ and the church."*** When Adam saw Eve, he recognized that she had been part of **his own body**. ***"This is now bone of my bones and flesh of my flesh."*** (Gen. 2:23) This speaks prophetically of the Church becoming *"one body,"* with **Jesus** as the Head.

---

[20] Eisenberg, *The JPS Guide*, 555-557.

[21] Kaplan, *Made in Heaven*, 83.

[22] Maurice Lamm, *The Jewish Way in Love and Marriage* (Middle Village: Jonathan David, 1980), 186-187.

In Jewish tradition, a wife's body is like a part of her husband's. They also teach that a man should love his wife like his own body.[23] Paul agreed with this ancient rabbinic understanding and connected it to Jesus and the Church, *"In this same way, **husbands ought to love their wives as their own bodies. He who loves his wife loves himself.** After all, no one ever hated their own body, but they feed and care for their body, **just as Christ does the church.**"* (Eph. 5:28-29 NIV) That means we must LOVE and care for our wives, but spiritually for the Bride, it's speaking about love in our relationships with other members of the Body of Christ.

Paul tells us that marriage mysteriously speaks about Jesus and His Church. I want to leave you with several thoughts that are connected to that idea. **First, we should remember that Adam and Eve were created in perfection.** They were sinless until the Fall. The perfect intent of God was that together, they would relate closely with each other and closely with Him. In Christ, we are able to approach the Lord and each other without sin or shame. This innocent and guileless interaction is critical for our relationship with the Lord. **Adam and Eve's innocence, in their shared relationship with God, is intended to be a prototype for the Bridal Company of Christ. We must be guiltless in relating to each other and to Jesus.**

Second, **Adam and Eve were not complete without each other.** That's why the Bible said, in marriage, they could once again become *"one flesh."* This speaks to the corporate nature of the Bride of Christ. Jesus said that the two most important commandments were to **love the Lord** and to **love your neighbor as yourself.** He then went on to say that the intent of the entire Bible was contained in those two related commandments.[24] This points us back to the Lord's initial plans for us to love Him as we love each other.

---

[23] Kaplan, *Made in Heaven*, 12.

[24] Matt. 22:37-40 ***Jesus replied: "Love the Lord your God** with all your heart and with all your soul and with all your mind.' This is the first and greatest commandment. And*

We are supposed to relate to God and to each other in **a holy love triangle,** comprised of ourselves and the Lord. **Jesus** is the Head and we are the Body. **Jesus** is the Bridegroom and we are the Bride of Christ. We are serving Him on earth together with every other member of the Bridal Company of Christ. Most of us are missing the corporate component of our relationship with the Lord. **The Church will not become the Bride *"made ready,"* until we embrace this.**

We were created to be in relationship with God and with other Christians. There should be no Lone Rangers in the Bride of Christ. As an introvert, I personally struggle with the human part of this equation. For me, it's difficult to bring other people into my relationship with the Lord. The personal stories I've included in this book invade my sense of privacy and stretch me, but I know this is one of the ways the Lord links us together. **We must work together to become who we are supposed to be.** If we want to become what Jesus has called for His Bride to be, that includes working closely with other Christians.

All marriage is ordained to be between a man, a woman, and God. If God is missing from the marriage, things are not as they were intended. Relationships in the Body of Christ are supposed to be between Christians in joint interaction with the Lord. If those components are not in place, we're not ready for the return of Jesus Christ. We need to help other believers advance in their relationships with each other and the Lord. If we advance, they should be blessed. If they advance, we're blessed. The intent of Heaven is that we would love each other and help each other to advance together. **May the Bride of Christ rise up to fulfill the dreams and intentions of our Creator. May we find our way back to the way it was *in the beginning*.**

---

the second is like it: 'Love your neighbor as yourself.' All the Law and the Prophets hang on these two commandments." NIV

Chapter 5:

Rebekah, the Willing Bride

Nobody comes into this world as part of the Bride of Christ, and you cannot become a true Christian under compulsion. On July 20, 1971, I was presented with the Lord's marriage proposal in the form of a salvation message at a *Young Life Camp*. I *willingly* chose to accept it and become born again. I immediately professed my new-found faith before many witnesses. After my salvation experience, I began a journey of discipleship, guided by the Holy Spirit, which continues to this very day. As Christians, **we must be willing** to leave our old life and follow the Lord. When we accept Jesus as our Lord and Savior, we begin a lifelong process that will ultimately lead us into eternity with Christ.

In Genesis 24, we find an aging Abraham who sends his trusted servant to seek a wife for his son Isaac. The servant finds Rebekah and determines that she is the perfect candidate. He then approaches her family with an offer of marriage, acting as an agent for Isaac. **Rebekah is asked if she will go** with the servant to become Isaac's wife, because she has to be **a *willing* bride**.[25] When asked by her brother and her mother, she enthusiastically agrees to the marriage.

---

[25] Gen. 24:58 *So they called Rebekah and asked her, "Will you go with this man?" "I will go," she said.* NIV

The servant gave **costly gifts** to her family and to Rebekah, securing the betrothal. The family **spoke a blessing** over Rebekah and sent her on her way. Rebekah then began a journey, guided by Abraham's servant, that ultimately led to Isaac and her new home. When she saw Isaac, **she veiled her face** before meeting him. Isaac brought her into his mother's **tent** and consummated the previously agreed marriage. There is great typology here for the Bride of Christ.

This is the story of the first Jewish wedding. Isaac was the first natural-born Jew, and Rebekah the Gentile married him in the prototypical wedding process. The sages tell us that many customs that came out of this wedding are still in use today. I'll explain several of these customs in more depth later, but for now I just want to mention some of them.

Abraham's servant acted as a matchmaker, still used in some Jewish traditions and now known as a *"shadkhan."* Some may remember this role as it was portrayed in the famous movie and play, *Fiddler on the Roof.* After locating the potential bride, the consent of her family is sought; the bride's family is approached by the matchmaker/servant and they discuss the prospects of a marriage. Also biblically known as *"the Friend of the Bridegroom,"* the *shadkhan* acts as an agent representing the groom and his family. A general discussion of the potential marriage takes place. If everything is positive to this point, the young lady will be asked if she is **willing** to marry the proposed groom.

Rebekah was evaluated for her suitability as a potential bride. Abraham's servant had set out to find an ideal wife for Isaac, and he prayed that God would guide him to the right woman. He specifically prayed the words, *"May it be that when I say to a young woman, 'Please let down your jar that I may have a drink,' and she says, 'Drink, and I'll water your camels too' — let her be the one you have chosen for your servant Isaac."*[26] Of course Rebekah met the requirements of this prayer request and became the prototype for all good Jewish wives.

---

[26] Gen. 24:14 May *it be that when I say to a young woman, 'Please let down your jar that I may have a drink,' and she says, 'Drink, and I'll water your camels too' — let her be*

The rabbis identify three critical characteristics from this passage and others, about Rebekah. She demonstrated **compassion** for the servant and his camels, **modesty/humility** in her dealings with the servant and **kindness/hospitality** in all of her interaction with him.[27] These are universally recognized virtues that are not exclusive to females. Like Rebekah, you will be tested. These same traits of **compassion, humility and kindness** are identified with Jesus in the New Testament. As part of the Bride of Christ, you should exhibit them in your life as well.

The *shadkhan* negotiated the bride for Isaac, and when the deal was struck, he gave her and her family valuable gifts. This gave biblical authority to two more marriage customs: the paying of a **Bride Price** to the bride's family and the giving of a gift to the bride, thereby securing the betrothal. The gift that was given as a present to the bride became known as *"kiddushin."* In Old Testament times, a bridal present/*kiddushin* was always given to the bride by the family of the groom as part of the formalities. This gift was usually a small silver or gold coin signifying that the purchase of the bride had been completed. Giving one coin to secure the betrothal, eventually evolved into our custom of giving an engagement ring.[28] By accepting the *kiddushin*, the bride was agreeing to the terms of the marriage.

The modern marriage tradition of **Seven Wedding Blessings (*Sheva Berakhot*)**, finds its roots in Rebekah's family blessing her and her pending union.[29] Rebekah put on a **veil** before approaching Isaac, which gave rise to bridal veiling that is still practiced today. (Gen. 24:65) Some point to Isaac taking Rebekah into his mother's **tent** as the origin of the *huppah* that is used as a **wed-**

---

the one you have chosen for your servant Isaac. By this I will know that you have shown kindness to my master." NIV

[27] Lamm, *The Jewish Way*, 98.

[28] Eisenberg, *The JPS Guide*, 43.

[29] Gen. 24:60 *And **they blessed** Rebekah.* NIV

ding canopy in many Jewish weddings. Many authorities feel that all of these customs are connected in some way to the marriage of Rebekah, but **I want to focus on her willingness to become Isaac's bride.**

The entire encounter, negotiation and acceptance by Rebekah was witnessed by family. *"So they called Rebekah and asked her, 'Will you go with this man?' 'I will go,' she said."* (Gen. 24:58 NIV) Notice that she said she was **willing** to become Isaac's bride and her mother and brother were witnesses. This verse gave rise to the requirement of two witnesses being needed to assure that the bride gave her consent to the union **without compulsion.** Pointing to the consent of Rebekah, witnessed by her brother and mother, Rabbi Maurice Lamm said that the primary reason witnesses are used in Jewish weddings to this day is to testify to the woman's willing consent. He also went on to say, **"Consent is the fundamental requirement of the wedding. There is no valid marriage without the total willing consent of the bride."** [30] Even in the weddings I perform in my present role as a pastor, we must have at least two witnesses who can testify to the willingness of both parties, for a legal union.

Now let's try to tie all of this Old Testament symbolism to the Bride of Christ. Christians sometimes point to the marriage of **Isaac** and **Rebekah** as a type of the relationship between **Jesus and the Church.** In this analogy, Isaac's father **Abraham** is symbolic of **God the Father, Isaac** is symbolic of **Jesus, Rebekah** is symbolic of **the Bride of Christ,** and **the unnamed servant** of Abraham is symbolic of the **Holy Spirit's work in facilitating our relationship with Jesus.**

It's not difficult to see Isaac's father **Abraham as a type of God the Father.** In Genesis 17:5 the *Amplified Bible* explains that *"Abram"* means *"high, exalted father."* God later changed his name to *"Abraham,"* which means *"father of a*

---

[30] Lamm, *The Jewish Way*, 153-154 and 163.

multitude." We can see direct connections to **God the Father** who is called the *"Father of all mankind."*[31]

Isaac is a type of Christ. Abraham and his wife Sarah, were unable to have children. Isaac's birth was supernatural; a shadow of Jesus being supernaturally implanted in the womb of the Virgin Mary by an act of God. In Genesis 22, Isaac is called Abraham's only son, like Jesus was later to be called God's only Son. (John 3:16) The Lord required Abraham to offer Isaac as a sacrifice. (Gen. 22:2) When the Lord finds that Abraham is willing to make the sacrifice of his only son, He provides a substitute for him. Christians see this as foreshadowing what God would do for mankind as He Himself would one day offer His only Son Jesus, as mankind's substitutionary sacrifice. Of course, Isaac was spared from death, but the typology is unmistakable. Like Jesus, Isaac is also heir to all that his father has. (Gen. 24:36)

The analogy is imperfect, but the unnamed servant of Abraham demonstrates some of the **nature and function of the Holy Spirit.** Some think he is Eliezer of Damascus, mentioned in Genesis 15:2, but the servant is given no personal name when he's sent to seek a bride for Isaac in Genesis 24. The Holy Spirit is never given a personal name in Scripture. Notice that he is sent to find a bride for Isaac, not for himself. The Holy Spirit draws men to Jesus and never promotes Himself. The servant is told to take a bride from among the family of Abraham (Gen. 24:4), and the Holy Spirit seeks the Bride of Christ only from the family of the redeemed. The servant ultimately guides Rebekah in a long journey to her new husband, and in a similar way, the Holy Spirit guides us in our lifetime journey and ultimate union with Jesus.

In the marriage of Isaac and Rebekah, **you are typified by Rebekah.** The Holy Spirit sought you from among mankind and offered you a sacred union with Jesus. You heard the plan of redemption and willingly agreed to follow the Lord.

---

[31] Eph. 4:6 *There is one God and **Father of all people**, who is Lord of all.* TEV

Rebekah (*representing every individual, including YOU*) had to WILLINGLY agree to accept the marriage proposal (*Gospel message*) and become betrothed to Isaac (*Jesus*). This speaks of the personal decision we all must make to become followers of Christ. We must each hear the proposal and willingly accept or reject it. This requires our understanding of what's intended and our willing agreement. Individually, we must be willing to become part of the Bride of Christ.

Finally, the Bride's willing decision to marry was not acceptable unless it could be affirmed by witnesses. To be valid, the commitment had to be verbalized. This speaks of your mandate to *acknowledge Jesus before mankind* by the *confession of your mouth*.

> **Matt. 10:32** *"Whoever acknowledges me before others, I will also acknowledge before my Father in heaven."* NIV

> **Rom. 10:9-10b** *"If you declare with your mouth, 'Jesus is Lord,' and believe in your heart that God raised him from the dead, you will be saved...and it is with your mouth that you profess your faith and are saved."* NIV

Nobody becomes a true born-again Christian under compulsion. **The Bride of Christ is *exclusively* made up of those who *willingly* acknowledge Jesus as their Bridegroom and confess Him before others.** For your marriage commitment to be valid in the eyes of God and man, there must be witnesses who can testify. **May you always live openly as a Christian, walking worthy of the price Jesus paid.**

CHAPTER 6:

Ruth's Kinsman-Redeemer

The entire book of *Ruth* is about a courtship and a marriage. Some contend that *Ruth* was written primarily to fill an important link in King David's genealogy and that of Jesus, the future Messiah, known as the Son of David. Along with the books of **Esther, Song of Solomon** and **Hosea, Ruth** was written about mankind's relationship with God, explained in the context of a human romance and marriage.

Ruth, a poor, young widow, meets and marries Boaz, a wealthy relative of her late husband. **The relationship between Boaz and Ruth can be viewed as symbolic of God's relationship with Israel, with Boaz representing the Lord and Ruth representing Israel; but it also speaks prophetically about Christ and His Bride** in several unusual ways.

After her husband's death in Moab, Ruth's mother-in-law, Naomi, tries to get her to return to her own family. When Naomi attempts to send her back, Ruth expresses her deep devotion to her and to Israel's God. She promised Naomi she would not leave her. The following words from Ruth are still used today as a pledge for converts to Judaism. These same words can also make a good addition to wedding vows.

Ruth 1:16 *"Ruth replied, 'Don't urge me to leave you or to turn back from you.* ***Where you go I will go, and where you stay I will stay. Your people will be my people and your God my God. 17 Where you die I will die, and there I will be buried. May the Lord deal with me, be it ever so severely, if even death separates you and me.'"*** NIV

Notice that Ruth pledged, ***"Your people will be my people,"*** implicitly stating that she was aligning herself with **ALL Jewish People** and not just Naomi. This speaks to the corporate responsibility each Jew was intended to assume for all other Jews. **Prophetically, for Christians, it speaks of our individual allegiance to all members of the corporate Bride of Christ.**

Naomi and Ruth then return from Moab to **Bethlehem**, the birthplace of Jesus, where the story unfolds. Ruth becomes the caretaker of her aging mother-in-law. She's an insignificant Gentile girl, living in Israel, with very poor future prospects. She dutifully works picking up leftover grain to make provision for herself and Naomi. One day, she works a particular field and attracts the favor of the owner, named Boaz, who is a rich and well-respected community leader. Boaz has heard the story of the virtuous, young Moabite widow. He gives instructions to his servants to make sure she's protected and well-provided for. When she tells Naomi that she has found favor with Boaz, Naomi explains that he is the close relative of Ruth's late husband, and he could act as her ***"Kinsman-Redeemer,"*** if he were willing to marry her. (Ruth 2:20 NIV)

Under Jewish Law, there were four requirements for a man to act as a kinsman-redeemer. The person had to be a blood relative of the deceased husband (kinsman); they had to have the resources to buy back any forfeited inheritance, such as lands, etc.; they had to be willing to carry out any legal responsibilities, like paying off debts; and, most importantly, they had to agree to marry the woman being *"redeemed"* and try to produce a male child with them to keep the family name alive. After being approached by Ruth about his potential responsibility, Boaz publicly declares his willingness to act in this role of kinsman-redeemer by saying, *"**Ruth** the Moabitess...have **I purchased to be my wife.**"* (Ruth 4:10 KJV)

Moabites were historically idolaters, and because of their terrible treatment of the Jews during the Exodus, they were forbidden from entering into the family of Israel for ten generations. (Deut. 23:3) Boaz didn't pay **the Bride Price for Ruth** so she could become his alien-born, idolatrous slave. She was redeemed to become his *wife*, with all of the normal privileges implied, along with access to Israel's God. Together, they ultimately became the ancestors of King David and later Joseph, the human father of Jesus. (Matt. 1:5-16)

There are several Jewish wedding customs that appear in this story. First, Ruth asked Boaz to *"**Spread your robe over your handmaid**"* (Ruth 3:9 CJB), in that way signifying his willingness to marry her. Many see this practice as a predecessor to the *huppah* ceremony that is still used to this day.[32] Second, Boaz announced *"**Ruth...I have purchased to be my wife.**"* (Ruth 4:10) This bridal "purchase" is sometimes pointed to as corroboration for the practice of paying **a Bride Price**. Third, to be valid under Jewish Law, the willingness of the parties involved in a marriage must be confirmed by qualified Jewish witnesses. The following verse gives support to that practice, *"Then the elders and all the people at the gate said, "**We are witnesses.**"* (Ruth 4:11a NIV) Those same elders then blessed the new couple,[33] giving weight to the tradition of public **Marriage Blessings** still found in Jewish weddings to this day.

Christians see **Naomi,** in guiding Ruth into her union with Boaz, **functioning as a type of the Holy Spirit. Boaz** can be looked at as a **type of Christ,**

---

[32] Also see Chapter 5, *Rebekah, the Willing Bride* and Chapter 9, *The Wedding at Mount Sinai* for more on *Huppahs*.

[33] Ruth 4:11 *May the Lord make the woman who is coming into your home like Rachel and Leah, who together built up the house of Israel. May you have standing in Ephrathah and be famous in **Bethlehem**. 12 Through the offspring the Lord gives you by this young woman, may your family be like that of Perez, whom Tamar bore to Judah.* NIV

and **Ruth** can be viewed as a **type of the Bride of Christ**. The story, significantly, is set in Bethlehem, where Jesus was later to be born. Ruth first joins herself to Naomi the Jew, then converts to following Israel's God. Most Christians were not born Jews, and they had to "convert" to become followers of their Jewish Messiah. Ruth is tested for her virtue. After we become followers of Jesus, we all must be *"tested and approved in Christ."* (Rom. 16:10) She has nothing of substance to offer, but Boaz is a rich and powerful leader. The Bible teaches that Jesus is the Creator and owner of all things (Col. 1:16), and each of us comes to Christ with nothing to bring Him but our love. **Ruth marries Boaz, who is her kinsman-redeemer, and Jesus is the Kinsman-Redeemer of mankind.**

Jesus came as a man (our *"blood"* relative), to pay the price for our sins and to redeem us from among men. Only Jesus had the legal ability to take back mankind's forfeited inheritance from the devil, because He lived as a man and didn't sin. He was willing to do what only He could do. Just as Boaz paid a price to redeem Ruth as his wife, Jesus was willing to pay the Bride Price for His Bride. In the case of Christ, the price was paid in His own blood.

Jesus redeemed you, and He's made you part of His Bridal Company. Like the poor Moabitess, Ruth, you probably were not born as part of Israel, and you had no access to the God of Abraham, Isaac and Jacob. Jesus extended kindness by giving you access to His Father. He purchased you to share in all that His Father has given to Him. (Luke 12:32) Christ redeemed you from sin and death, not just so you could escape judgment; He wants to have you as His companion forever. And, by His grace, I'll be there too.

There is a fascinating conclusion to the love story of Ruth and Boaz. They met in Bethlehem and lived there until the time of their deaths. The Hebrew name of Bethlehem is *Bet Lehem*, which means *"House of Bread."* Their traditional home stayed in the family and later became the birthplace and early home of King David. This is where Samuel came to anoint young David as king. (1 Sam. 16:1-3) David probably lived there when he slew Goliath. By the first century, the family property had been converted to an inn. The ruins of their old home became a small stable that was carved out of a natural depression in rock. This stable, or manger, later became the **birthplace of Jesus Christ,** *the Bread of Life.*[34]

> **Matt. 1:5** *"Boaz the father of Obed, whose mother was* **Ruth***, Obed the father of Jesse, 6 and Jesse the father of King David. David was the father of Solomon, whose mother had been Uriah's wife…16 and Jacob the father of Joseph, the husband of Mary, and Mary was the mother of* **Jesus** *who is called the Messiah."* NIV

---

[34] This is an old tradition, mentioned by Henry H. Halley, *Halley's Bible Handbook,* 24th ed. (Grand Rapids: Zondervan, 1965), *176.,* commenting on Ruth Chapter 4, and Merrill F. Unger, *Unger's Bible Handbook* (Chicago: Moody Press, 1965), 514. commenting on Luke Chapter 2.

CHAPTER 7:

Esther and the Lion King

Some years ago, the Lord called me to Bible School. While I was there, a visiting preacher spoke a message from the following verse in *Esther*:

> Esther 2:12 *"Each young woman's turn came to go in to King Ahasuerus after she had completed twelve months' preparation."* NKJV

The speaker was **Tommy Tenney**, who later wrote *One Night With the King* based on the book of *Esther*. He's a great preacher, and he shared many things in his message that impacted me and influenced my thinking. As I remember, he simply told the story of the Jewish orphan Esther and how she became queen of the Persian Empire. He said at some point, that Esther had the smell of the poor on her, and she needed time to be prepared to smell like a King's bride. Tenney pointed out the necessity for **Esther's time of preparation** and said that it was similar to our life of preparation in becoming part of the Bride of Christ.

As I considered his words, the Lord spoke to me, **"I brought you to Bible School to get the smell of the world off of you."** At that time, I was in my early 40s, and I'd been in part-time ministry for many years. It sometimes seemed that

I already knew what they were teaching me at Bible School. Just as Esther needed a time of preparation to learn the ways of King Ahasuerus, the Lord sent me to Bible School, primarily because I needed more time for preparation to learn the ways of King Jesus. **To the world, I already looked like a preacher, but to the Lord, I smelled like the world.**

The story of Esther opens as King Ahasuerus invites his wife Vashti to a feast and she refuses to come. (Esther 1:12) Vashti loses her position as the king's wife because of her unwillingness to respond to his invitation, and a new bride is sought for the king. (Esther 1:19) A great contest is held, seeking the most beautiful and virtuous young woman in the entire kingdom to become a bride for King Ahasuerus. **Esther** is a poor, Jewish orphan, living with her cousin, Mordecai. He instructs her to enter the contest as a candidate for becoming the new queen. She is then guided by Mordecai and the King's servant, Hegai, during **her days of preparation.** She is given beauty treatments and taught how to please the king, and how to one day live with him as his wife. (Esther 2:8-15) Under their direction, Esther prepares herself well, obtains favor, and is ultimately married to King Ahasuerus. (Esther 2:17)

The second act of this story begins after Esther becomes queen. The king has a very powerful advisor named Haman, who serves as a sort of prime minister in the kingdom. Haman is an evil man who hates Esther's cousin Mordecai, but does not know that they're related. Haman finds out that Mordecai is a Jew, and, unsatisfied with killing just him, he gets permission to kill every Jew in the Persian Empire. Mordecai is told of the plot and sends word to Queen Esther of what Haman has planned.

Esther was at first reluctant to approach the king about this matter, because Persian court protocol forbade it under penalty of death. Mordecai responded to her reluctance with these words,

Esther 4:13b-14 *"Do not think that because you are in the king's house **you alone of all the Jews** will escape. **For if you remain silent at this time, relief and deliverance for the Jews will arise from another place**, but you and your father's family will perish. **And who knows but that you have come to your royal position for such a time as this?"** NIV*

Mordecai pointed out her responsibility to her people in the verse above, saying that God would use her for their defense or choose someone else. Queen Esther rose to the challenge and responded appropriately, just as the good Jewish girl she was, by saying, *"I will go to the king, even though it is against the law. And if I perish, I perish."* (Esther 4:16 NIV) Esther **realized that God had elevated her, for the good of ALL Jewish people.** She assumed responsibility for the corporate people of God, at the risk of her own life. She was then able to approach the king without any problem, because of her position of favor. She made her case, and the king dispensed with his evil advisor, Haman, making Mordecai his replacement. With Mordecai's help, they destroyed Haman's plan to kill all the Jews and ultimately preserved the people of God.

Esther is primarily a book about the Lord's divine protection for the Jewish people from an evil opponent seeking to destroy them. **For Christians**, rich typology can be found in this Old Testament book when it is seen through the lens of the New Testament. The Persian king **Ahasuerus** is the ruler of the known world, and his name means *"Lion King."*[35] His empire is shown as being incredibly vast and powerful. Even though he is a pagan, in some respects, he

---

[35] William Gesenius, *Gesenius Hebrew-Chaldee Lexicon of the Old Testament*, (Grand Rapids: Baker Book House, 1979), 34. The king's name "Ahasuerus" is derived from a Hebrew translation of his Persian name. "Xerxes" is used in many translations and it comes from the Greek version of his Persian name. Gesenius tells us that his Persian name means **"lion king."**

is a type of **the all-powerful King Jesus,** who is called *the Lion of the Tribe of Judah* in *Revelation 5:5.*

The king's first wife, **Vashti,** is a type of **Israel** in the first century. Queen Vashti rejected the king's invitation, and this made room for a new queen to be chosen. King Jesus came first to the Jewish people, whom God had married at Mount Sinai. Even though many individual Jews believed on Him, their leadership collectively rejected Him. Queen Vashti's offense speaks prophetically of Israel's initial rejection of Christ as their Bridegroom. Paul explained that their rejection of Christ opened the Kingdom to the Gentiles. This is similar to the New Testament parable of *the Wedding of the King's Son* where Jesus speaks of Israel being invited to a wedding feast and refusing to come, so others were then invited. (Matt. 22:2-14) I should add that the analogy is flawed, because many first century Jews did receive Jesus and Israel is still chosen to be married to the Lord; but the prophetic comparisons are still valid.

Esther is guided by her cousin **Mordecai and the king's steward, Hegai.** In a similar manner, the **Holy Spirit** guides us. Mordecai initiated the process for Esther to become the king's bride and guided the progression of events. **The Holy Spirit convicts us of our need for Jesus and guides us along the way.** Mordecai continued to watch over Esther and advise her, even after she had become Queen. **The Holy Spirit leads us to Jesus, and He is with us even after we are saved, continually directing our lives. Hegai** was given the task of preparing Esther for marriage with the king and teaching her the protocols of the kingdom. In a similar way, **the Holy Spirit prepares us for King Jesus and teaches us the protocols of the Kingdom of Heaven.**[36]

Esther, the poor orphan, is a type of the **Bride of Christ.** She is selected to become **the new bride of the great Lion King.** Her lack of social standing points to our condition as mere human beings who are called into an immortal

---

[36] For sources and an extended look at the Person and work of the Holy Spirit, I submit John 14-16 and Romans 8.

union with our Creator and Bridegroom. **This is a beautiful love story,** where a poor girl with few prospects, marries the greatest king on earth, and together they overcome an evil adversary. **Esther/*Bride of Christ* marries Lion King/ Jesus,** and together they overcome **Haman/*Satan*.**

Esther's wicked opponent **Haman,** is obviously a type of **Satan. Haman** wants to kill Esther and all of her Jewish people. (Esther 3:5-6) She must stand against Haman to triumph over evil and please the Lord, just as we must stand against the devil. (Esther 4:14) Ultimately, Esther and the king destroy the evil Haman, along with all of his evil allies, and they live happily ever after. (Esther 7:6-10:3) This speaks of the ultimate destruction of Satan and our eternal destination with Jesus in paradise. (Rev. 20:10) It also serves as a reminder to Jew and Gentile alike, that no Haman, Hitler or Ahmadinejad will ever be able to destroy God's Jewish people.

Ten different feasts are mentioned in the book of Esther. I won't review them all, but it is relevant to mention a few of them. The story opens with the great king hosting a seven-day feast for the nobles of his kingdom. He invites Queen Vashti, who refuses to come and is in the middle of hosting her own feast. Later, Queen Esther gives two feasts for the king and Haman, with Haman exposed and judged at the second one. The last chapters feature victory feasts for the Jewish people of Persia to celebrate Esther's victory over Haman. This national Jewish victory becomes *the Feast of Purim*, celebrated to this day in remembrance of Esther's story. **In our Bride of Christ prophetic analogy, these feasts all point to the *Marriage Feast of the Lamb*.** (Rev. 19:9) In that great Wedding Feast, the faithful from all ages will join together with the great Lion King Jesus to celebrate His Bride's victory over the devil and the kingdoms of this world.

In addition to the typology for the Bride of Christ, there are several things I want us to take away from the book of *Esther*. First, Esther was called as a potential bride for the ruler of the known world. **You are called to be in a similar**

relationship with Jesus, King of Kings and ruler of all. Esther did not come from royalty, and she needed a full year to be prepared to relate to the King. You were born mortal, and you didn't come into the Kingdom knowing the ways of our eternal God. The Bible teaches that we enter into a relationship with Jesus when we commit our lives to Him, but we still need to be prepared to live with Him. **Esther needed only one year of preparation, but you will need a lifetime.** The Holy Spirit helps us and teaches us the ways of the King. We must rely on the Holy Spirit to show us the protocol of the courts of heaven.

Esther was put on this earth to know God and do His will. Her destiny was not simply for advancement on this earth. Mordecai expressed it this way, *"For if you keep silent at this time, relief and deliverance shall arise for the Jews from elsewhere, but you and your father's house will perish. And **who knows but that you have come to the kingdom for such a time as this** and for this very occasion?"* (Esther 4:14 AMP) Each of us *comes to the kingdom for such a time as this,* meaning that we are each called to use our influence in the world for the purposes of God. If you keep silent when it is time to speak up for the Lord, God will still have His way, but you'll miss your destiny. **Like Queen Esther, whoever you are, whatever you do, and whoever you know, it is for the glory of God.** There will be many occasions to remember this lesson.

Finally, I want to conclude this chapter by sharing a dream I had on March 1, 2008, that was a bit reminiscent of the Narnia stories and their featured Lion King, Aslan.

In the dream, I was staying in a 2nd row beach hotel with my two daughters, Courtney and Rachael. We were attending some type of Christian Conference, and I was getting more and more frustrated because I wasn't getting anything from the Lord. Rachael went home, but Courtney and I stayed. I got more frustrated and decided to leave. I went for a walk from the hotel, across to the beach, to tell everyone I was leaving. Everyone else attending the conference was already at the beach. For some reason, I had to walk through the repair bay of a gas station to get to the beach. That was my only point of access to the beach.

As I went into the repair bay, the ocean was in front of me, and there were two large, male African lions behind a wire grate. They were very fierce, and they were growling at me. Somehow the two lions got loose. There was a big double bed next to me on my left in the repair bay. I jumped up on the bed trying to get away from the lions. They were still growling and eyeing me fiercely. One moved away, but one of the lions jumped up on the bed beside me. He began to nuzzle me playfully and make soft noises like a house cat. I slowly realized he was not going to harm me and he was really happy to be with me. End of dream.

When I awoke, I was struck with several of the images from the dream. I was at a *"Christian Conference,"* but it wasn't touching my heart. Intimacy with the Lord is what I'm always after, and that's not normally found in a conference. Intimacy with Jesus comes from being alone with Jesus. I thought to leave, but I encountered a lion. The lion was certainly powerful enough to hurt me, but he was very gentle, even playful with me. The image of me and the lion on the double bed struck me as significant, in a non-sexual, but intimate way.

I came away with a fresh understanding of the Lion of Judah. To the Lost of this world, **Jesus** seems fierce and will one day be quite frightening, but to us He is gentle as a Lamb. To the world, **Jesus** seems distant and aloof, but to us He's seeking intimacy that He often compares to that found in marriage. As part of the waiting Bride of Christ, **the rest of our days will be spent preparing** to spend eternity with **King Jesus, the Lion of the Tribe of Judah.** Each of us has come into the Kingdom, for such a time as this.

We need the Holy Spirit to guide our lifetime of preparation. The Holy Spirit will help you get free from the smell of this world. If you submit to His guidance, the Holy Spirit will prepare you to function as the eternal companion of the King of Kings. As you yield to this process, **He will show you what you'll need to live with Jesus as His Bride.** Together with Jesus, you will overcome Satan. **To you, the Lion *King* of the Tribe of Judah is the Lamb of God, and you are His Chosen Bride.**

CHAPTER 8:

Solomon's Song

When I told a Jewish friend that I was writing a book about the Bride of Christ, she immediately assumed it was based on the *Song of Solomon*. When most people think of romance in the Bible, the *Song of Solomon* is the only book that comes to mind. It conveys the romantic story of King Solomon, who sings his love song to the poor Shulamite/Bride, as she sings her love song to him.

This book is also known as *Song of Songs*, and it has traditionally been understood by many religious Jews to be an allegory of human romance that also speaks about the Lord's relationship with Israel.[37] One modern Jewish scholar has expressed the rabbinic understanding this way, *"Song of Songs...is a metaphor for God's love for Israel and Israel's love for God."*[38] Another scholar, seeing even deeper significance within the pages, said, *"It speaks of the highest spiritual levels to which a mortal can aspire. It is taught that if all the books of the Bible are holy, then the Song of Songs is holy of holies."*[39]

The *Song of Solomon* speaks first about the relationship between the Lord and Israel and secondarily about the Lord Jesus and the Bride of Christ. We see

---

[37] Eisenberg, *The JPS Guide*, 29.

[38] Jacob Neusner, *A Midrash Reader* (Minneapolis: Fortress Press, 1990), 142.

[39] Kaplan, *Made in Heaven*, 9.

King Solomon as a type of Jesus and the Shulamite as a type of the redeemed individual and the entire Bride of Christ. The imagery within the book is sometimes romantically graphic, yet it is also laced with subtle meaning. The name *"Solomon"* means *"peaceful."* The Messiah/Christ was prophesied to be the **Prince of Peace.** (Isa. 9:6) The woman, who is the object of the king's favor, is called *"Shulamite,"* which means *"daughter of peace"* or *"one who found peace."*[40] Jesus came as the Prince of Peace, and He said that He would bring peace to His Bride when He proclaimed, *"Peace I leave with you; my peace I give you."* (John 14:27)

As in the stories of *Rebekah, Esther* and *Ruth,* the Shulamite attracts the attention of a powerful man. In each case, the wealthy bridegroom condescends to find his bride from among those who can never hope to ascend to his social status. In *Song of Solomon,* **He is the son of David and the ruler of all Israel.** The great king pursues a poor, working-class bride who has no place among royalty. This speaks of our having no way to merit the love and favor of Christ, yet He graciously condescends to save us and enter into a marriage covenant with us.

I met the late **Wade E. Taylor** in March of 2002, and he became my dear friend and mentor until his death in February of 2012. He made a lasting impression on my life with his love for Jesus, his humility, and his playful good nature. Brother Wade wrote *"The Secret to the Stairs,"* which is a beautiful, mystic interpretation of the *Song of Solomon.* In that book, Taylor teaches that **Solomon (*the Son of David*) speaks as Jesus. The redeemed individual (*and Bridal Company of Christ*) is represented by the Shulamite.** He explains that she goes through a process of maturation, evidenced by three progressively less selfish declarations of love toward the Bridegroom.

In the first profession, the bride selfishly says, *"My beloved is mine, and I am his."* (Song. 2:16 KJV) Her first thought is possessive as she says *"He is*

---

[40] PC Study Bible, *Fausset's Bible Dictionary* (CD-ROM, 2007), on "Shulamite."

mine" and almost as an afterthought, *"and I am his."* The second profession shows some progress when she gives her position with her *beloved* top billing and says, *"I am my beloved's and my beloved is mine."* (Song. 6:3 KJV) The third and final profession of the mature bride shows the unselfish love of a life totally given over to another. *"I am my beloved's, and His desire is toward me."* (Song. 7:10 KJV) Taylor's point is that the Lord is looking for unselfish love from a Bridal Company that has matured and become totally committed to Jesus. Their greatest desire is to belong to the One who desires them.

I interviewed Wade about the *Song of Solomon* and the Bride of Christ in 2008. I've included a rather long portion of that interview, because I think it speaks marvelously to the entire concept of the Bride of Christ. As part of the question and answer session, I asked him to share some thoughts on the mature Bride's profession from *Song of Solomon 7:10, "I am my beloved's, and his desire is toward me."* This is an edited transcript of his words as they were recorded during that interview. It's far below the normal finished quality of his writing, but prior to his death, he graciously approved this version of his remarks for eventual publication in my book.

Pitts: "Wade, in your book, *"The Secret of the Stairs,"* you expound on part of a verse from *Song of Solomon*, *"I am my beloved's, and his desire is toward me."* (Song. 7:10 KJV) Please give me your thoughts on that particular verse."

Wade Taylor: "The following verse has fascinated me for years, and it is background for my thinking on *Song of Solomon* 7:10. I want to share this first, so I can put it in the right context. *'Deep calls to deep.'* (Ps. 42:7a) That verse speaks of an interaction with the Lord, *'Deep calls to deep.'* The first *'Deep'* is God calling with a capital *'D.'* God is a social Being. He created Adam singularly. We don't know how long Adam existed by himself, but the Lord realized that he was an incomplete creation. He took from Adam a counterpart to his life called *'woman'* (Gen. 2:22), and in the interaction of the two there came a completion.

"God is seeking interaction with man, **'Deep calls to deep.'** He created the universe itself with all of its vastness, but He couldn't find satisfaction in it. He created multitudes of angels and the hosts of Heaven, but He couldn't find satisfaction in His interaction with them. He created Adam with a free will and Eve as his counterpart to be his wife. The two together became the expression of His desire for a completion in Himself that He hadn't had with the previous beings of the created order. So, in the completion that came through Adam having a wife, God saw something that He desired.

"In the beginning of the *Song of Solomon*, the Shulamite said, I love you *'because of the savor of your good ointments.'* (Song. 1:3 KJV) In other words, I love you because of what you can do for me. She says, *'As the apple tree among the trees of the wood, so is my beloved.'* (Song. 2:3 KJV) *'Stay me with flagons; comfort me with apples.'* (Song. 2:5 KJV) These *'flagons'* and *'apples'* speak of her desire for blessings; in her immature love, she is focused on the things he can give her. The Lord said she was *'as a lily'* among all the other women. (Song. 2:1-2) In other words, He said *'You are one special lily among all the multiplied lilies of the field.'* That recognition of her unique identity and her unique qualities has to do with the favor of God.

"I can cultivate the favor of God, because God has favorites. Many preachers will say, *'God doesn't have any favorites,'* but He does. **'Deep calls to deep.'** (Ps. 42:7) There's such a thing as cultivating divine favor. We can obtain the approbation of God. This word *'approbation'* speaks of the Lord taking an interest in my life. I can live and move in such a way that the Lord becomes personally interested in me.

"This is the same principle that humans use in selecting a mate for marriage. Before we chose one, we are interested in the many. Before we marry, we are looking at the field. All at once your interest switches from the field to one, because something in her causes a response in you and it sticks. This is a unique response, and this special interest ends in a marriage. Now where did we get the ability to do that? Where did that ability come from? This came from the Lord.

"So, if we are created in His image and we got this ability to become uniquely aware and interested in one individual, then He has the same thing in Himself. Therefore, He is capable of choosing one from amongst all the redeemed of the world. He can pick out one and become personally interested in that person. This is the approbation or the favor of God, resting on one as though you were the only person in the universe.

"The Lord mentioned two different men in Scripture, Abraham and David, as being His friends in the sense of a unique friendship. There was something within each one that touched His heart. David, frequently under intense pressure, turned to the Lord every time, and it touched the heart of God. Abraham became the friend of God in a unique arrangement or calling. He chose God when he could have chosen something else. With just these two examples, we can see that there is such a thing as the favor of God resting on an individual.

"Now let's look at our key verse, *'I am my beloved's, and his desire is toward me.'* The statement, *'His desire is toward me'* has to do with a person who has cultivated God's favor. In the beginning she says, *'He feeds among the lilies.'* (Song. 2:16) In other words, *'Lord, in case I have a problem, the only thing I want to know is where you are.'* But she grew beyond that immature position. She progressed to the place where she became the apple of His eye and where He had a single eye towards her. She is like a *dove* (Song. 2:14), and He is like a *roe*. (Song. 2:9) That speaks of the Lord and the Bride. It's a two-way thing. It's expressed first one way, then the other.

"In another place, the Lord says, *'I love them that love me; and those that seek me early shall find me...That I may cause those that love me to inherit substance.'* (Prov. 8:17, 21a KJV) That is our response to His *'Deep'* calling, resulting in the favor of God resting on our life. These Biblical principles clearly reveal that there is such a thing as cultivating a unique relationship with God.

"*'I am my beloved's, and his desire is toward me.'* She says this because He touched something in her. There was something in her that wasn't satisfied with anything less than the Lord Himself. At first that wasn't true, but something happened in the progression of their relationship, and the favor of God began to rest on her life. See, *'Deep calls to deep.'* That desire called and found a response and fulfillment. That *'Deep calling'* is the desire of the heart of God. No angel could ever give the response the Lord desired, because it has to come from a person with free will. Unless we had the ability not to respond, we could never satisfy the heart of God. He is the *'Deep'* calling, and as **His Bride,** we are the *'deep'* who must respond." *End of Wade Taylor Interview.* [41]

In *"The Secret to the Stairs,"* Brother Wade points out that the Bride grows in her love from being very self-centered to being totally focused on the Lord. The Bride's first interest in the Bridegroom comes with the question, *"what can you do for me?"* This is very much like an immature Christian, who only prays with a list of wants for the Lord. The *Song of Solomon* progresses with the Bride slowly coming to realize that she has a good thing, simply because the Bridegroom is interested in her and He is worthy of her desire. Then, she moves beyond even that point and finds mature joy in the fact that, *"I am my beloved's, and His desire is toward me."* This response of love and unconditional surrender is characteristic of the Bride Jesus is seeking.

When I was fifteen, a close friend of mine wrote a song about the return of Jesus for His Bride, including the words, *"Rise up, my love, my fair one, and come away."* (Song. 2:10 KJV) His song sparked my first real interest in the concept of the Bride of Christ, and it had to do with my immature desire to break out from my earthly responsibilities. I would often sing Mike's song to the Lord and imagine Jesus singing those words over me, as He would come to carry me away from my fifteen-year-old trials and tribulations. I primarily wanted Jesus to

---

[41] Wade E. Taylor, *Personal Interview*, August 3, 2008.

come, so I could escape from life's temptations and troubles. I now know that was a very childish motivation, but the Lord was not put off. Even in my youth and immaturity, the seeds of desire to belong to Jesus were planted deeply in my heart.

In all the years that have followed, Hell could not put those seeds to death. The plan of the Lord has always been to identify those who desire Him as He desires them. I now know that **His desire for us far outweighs our greatest desire for Him.** He is the loving God who created us to be with Him, and nothing less will satisfy us. Jesus is coming for a willing Bride who longs for Him. For Christians, there will always be trouble in this life, but Jesus will never leave us or forsake us. For those who overcome, He will one day sing *His Song of Songs* over us, *"Arise my love, my fair one and come away."* The mature Bridal **Company of Christ is made up of those who only want to belong to Jesus.** For us, nothing else in this world matters. In the words of the Shulamite's ancient profession of love, we declare, *"I am my beloved's, and His desire is toward me."*

CHAPTER 9:

The Wedding At Mount Sinai

My mother's name was ***Beulah,*** which means ***"married"*** in Hebrew. It's used in *Isaiah,* where **the Lord promised to marry the land of Israel.**[42] This is where we get the expression ***"Beulah-land,"*** in speaking about **Israel.** From the earliest memories I have of my mother, I always knew that she loved the Lord. **My mother also deeply loved the Jewish people.** When I was a young child, she taught me that the Jewish people are *"the chosen people"* and the Lord's special nation. To Mom, the land of Israel was always, *"the Holy Land"* and **Jesus was her Jewish Messiah.** She inherited her love for God's chosen people from her mother, and that became part of her legacy to me. I've passed down that same love to my own children and grandchildren.

I'm very grateful that I was born into a Christ-centered family who taught us that God was not finished with Israel. The Bible clearly teaches that the Lord entered into a marriage relationship with the Jewish people, and they are His chosen. **Some don't believe that, but it's irrefutable and should be affirmed**

---

[42] Isa. 62:4 *No longer will they call you Deserted, or name your land Desolate. But you will be called Hephzibah, and your land **Beulah;** for the Lord will take delight in you, and **your land will be married.** 5 As a young man marries a young woman, so will your Builder marry you; as a **bridegroom rejoices over his bride, so will your God rejoice over you.** NIV*

and celebrated by every Bible-believing Christian. **God loves the Jews, and He is not finished with them.**

In the book of *Exodus,* we find that the Lord initiated a Marriage Covenant with the nation of Israel, through Moses. This marriage is alluded to in many places in the Bible, including the verses from the Prophets below.

> **Isa. 54:5** *"For your Maker is your husband — the Lord Almighty is his name — the Holy One of Israel is your Redeemer; he is called the God of all the earth."* NIV

> **Jer. 3:14** *"Return, faithless people,' declares the Lord, 'for I am your husband.'"* NIV

The rabbis have traditionally taught that Mount Sinai is where God extended the offer of Marriage to Israel and where they agreed to accept. Many Christian scholars concur with this understanding.[43]

The Christian writer, S.J. Hill tells us, *"According to Jewish tradition, the covenant God initiated with His people at Mount Sinai was really a covenant of marriage."* He goes on to say that the rabbis have believed for centuries that the Jewish wedding ceremony is a re-enactment of what happened at Sinai, and it reflects the primary features of God's covenant with Israel.[44] The Jews believe that the Lord gave Israel a marriage contract through Moses. The Hebrew word for **"marriage contract"** is *"ketubah,"* and it literally means *"written document."* There is traditionally a *ketubah* drawn up that details the terms of the marriage covenant. Many Jews understand *Exodus* and the entire *Torah* to be a marriage *ketubah* between God and Israel.

---

[43] Dr. Berin Gilfillan, *Personal Interview*, August 11, 2008.

[44] Hill, *Burning Desire*, 42.

Since the actual marriage ceremony is somewhat veiled, I want to give a short recap of the Exodus story with a view toward the marriage of God and Israel, from a Jewish perspective. God called Israel out of slavery into marriage with Himself, and He gave them the wealth of Egypt. (Ex. 3:21-22) The prophet Ezekiel later confirmed that the gold, silver and other articles they took out of Egypt were Bridal Gifts from the Lord that secured their betrothal to Him.[45] They moved en masse from Egypt to Mount Sinai, where the Lord used Moses as a matchmaker between Himself and the people. God told Moses to go tell all of the people what He had to say. (Ex. 19:3) The Lord then pledged His love and offered them a Marriage Covenant that would join the entire nation of Israel to Himself in a special relationship that was unique in all the earth. ***"Now therefore, if you obey my voice and keep my covenant, you shall be my treasured possession out of all the peoples. Indeed, the whole earth is mine, but you shall be for me a priestly kingdom and a holy nation."*** (Ex. 19:5-6 NRSV)

So, Moses began to go back and forth between God and Israel, negotiating the terms of their marriage and telling each of them what the other was saying. After hearing the initial terms, Israel took an oath saying, *"We will do everything the Lord has said."* (Ex. 19:8 NIV) Moses took their words back to the Lord, and He said, *"Great, I am coming down on the third day, so get them dressed and ready."* (Ex. 19:10–13, my own paraphrased version) Acting as the *Friend of the Bridegroom*, Moses led the people out of the camp on the third day to meet

---

[45] Ezek. 16:8 *And when I passed by again, I saw that you were old enough for love. So I wrapped my cloak around you to cover your nakedness and **declared my marriage vows**. I **made a covenant with you**, says the Sovereign Lord, and you became mine. 9 "Then I bathed you and washed off your blood, and I rubbed fragrant oils into your skin. 10 I gave you expensive clothing of fine linen and silk, beautifully embroidered, and sandals made of fine goatskin leather. 11 I gave you lovely jewelry, bracelets, beautiful necklaces, 12 a ring for your nose, earrings for your ears, and a lovely crown for your head. 13 And so you were adorned with gold and silver. Your clothes were made of fine linen and were beautifully embroidered. You ate the finest foods—choice flour, honey, and olive oil—and became more beautiful than ever. **You looked like a queen, and so you were!*** NLT

with God, and He was waiting there under a wedding canopy of fire, smoke and clouds. (Ex. 19:16-18) The Lord laid out His commandments and terms for the marriage, as is recorded in the next five chapters of *Exodus*.

In Exodus 24:3 *"Moses went and **told the people all the Lord's words and laws,"*** and after hearing them, they took another oath to do everything Moses had just laid out. *"Everything the Lord has said we will do."* Moses then wrote all that the Lord had said in a marriage contract, called *"The Book of the Covenant,"* and he read it to the people. After hearing the written terms of the Marriage Covenant, they once again gave an oath to abide by God's terms. (Ex. 24:7) This is how the rabbis traditionally view the Marriage Covenant given at Mount Sinai.

Because of this understanding, that Israel was married to God at Mount Sinai, there are a number of wedding customs that either come from the *Exodus* account or find additional support from it. For example, Jewish wedding ceremonies are performed under a wedding canopy called a *huppah*, that points back to the canopy of the sky over Mount Sinai that was made up of smoke, fire and lightening. There are other Biblical events that scholars believe also point to the *huppah* and its use in weddings, but the connection with Israel's marriage to God under the canopy of the sky at Sinai is among the oldest.

In traditional Jewish culture, the human agent who represents the bridegroom in negotiations with potential brides as a matchmaker, is often referred to as the *"Friend of the Bridegroom."* There is a strong rabbinic tradition that speaks of Moses as the *Friend of the Bridegroom* that God used to lead Israel into a marriage covenant with Him.[46] The Lord sent Moses back and forth, negotiating His marriage to the people of Israel. As mentioned above, many verses in Exodus show Moses performing this function, including the following: *"Then Moses led the people out of the camp to meet with God, and they stood at the foot of the mountain."* (Ex. 19:17)

---

[46] Edersheim, *Sketches*, 153.

A special *ketubah* (marriage contract) is sometimes read in Jewish services at Pentecost, because they celebrate Pentecost as the time of the giving of the *Torah* at Sinai as a *Marriage Covenant.* Oil lamps and candles were incorporated into the wedding procession to remind the people of God that the Lord had once come down in fire to be married to them at Mount Sinai.[47] This tradition comes from the fire and lightning that appeared on the sacred mountain in Exodus 19 and 24. The early Jewish disciples of Christ would likely have connected oil lamp flames with the custom of the Bridal lights, passed down from the marriage of the Lord to Israel at Sinai. Set in the context of a wedding, the parable of *the Wise and Foolish Virgins* in Matthew 25 makes use of Bridal oil lamps to make several points. Perhaps the Lord used fire on the day of Pentecost in Acts 2 to symbolically point to the marriage of the Church and Christ? Every member of the Bridal Company in the Upper Room received a personal flame from the Holy Spirit (Acts 2:3), who is also *the Friend of the Bridegroom.* **John the Baptist** clearly identified himself as *the Friend of the Bridegroom* when speaking of **Jesus as the Bridegroom** in John 3:29.

After the terms of the *ketubah* are read during the marriage ceremony, the Jewish bride and groom pledge before witnesses to abide by the details. This practice also comes from the book of Exodus and the Marriage between Israel and the Lord. The rabbis teach that the Lord's oath to Israel (His Bride) was, *"Now therefore, if ye will obey my voice indeed, and keep my covenant, then ye shall be a peculiar treasure unto me above all people."* (Ex. 19:5 KJV) After the Lord as Husband presents His vows, Israel the Bride then gives hers. Moses read the commandments/*ketubah* of the Lord, and the people of Israel publicly affirmed their intentions to abide by the Lord's terms of Marriage, *"Then he took the Book of the Covenant and read it to the people. They responded, "We will do everything the LORD has said; we will obey."* (Ex. 24:7 NIV)

---

[47] Eisenberg, *The JPS Guide,* 39.

Observant Jewish men began to wear a garment known as a *tallith* on their wedding day. The tallith is the traditional prayer garment with fringes, created as a fulfillment of the Lord's instructions in Numbers 15:37-40 and Deuteronomy 22:12. The tradition of the bridegroom's first use of a *tallith* on his wedding day, historically stems from an interesting belief that God was seen wearing one on His wedding day with Israel at Sinai. For scriptural support of what is believed to have been seen, they sometimes point to Psalm 104:2, *"He wraps himself in light as with a garment."* [48]

Wedding gifts, in the form of gold, silver or fine garments, are sometimes given to the Bride to secure the actual betrothal or as bridal gifts at the wedding ceremony. The rabbis teach that God gave Israel the wealth of Egypt as "tokens" to seal their betrothal to Him.[49] God seems to support this in the following passage from Ezekiel, where He gives us a long look at His view of the marriage between Himself and Israel, and He lists their wedding gifts.

> **Ezek. 16:10-13** *"I clothed you with an **embroidered dress** and put sandals of fine leather on you. I dressed you in **fine linen** and covered you with **costly garments**. I adorned you with **jewelry**: I put **bracelets** on your arms and a **necklace** around your neck, and I put a **ring** on your nose, **earrings** on your ears and a **beautiful crown** on your head. So you were adorned with **gold** and **silver**; your clothes were of **fine linen** and **costly fabric** and **embroidered cloth**."* NIV

After the father approved every preparation for the wedding, they would blow a *shofar* and the *Friend of the Bridegroom* would shout to announce the

---

[48] Kaplan, *Made in Heaven*, 55-56.

[49] Kaplan, *Made in Heaven*, 46.

wedding and notify the Bride and the guests that the Groom was coming. The wedding party would then go out to meet the Groom. The trumpet sounded loudly in Exodus 19, and Moses led the people out to meet the Lord. This may remind Christians of other trumpet blasts contained in the New Testament announcing the return of our Bridegroom, like the following, *"For **the Lord himself will come** down from heaven, with a loud command, with **the voice of the archangel** and with **the trumpet call of God**, and the dead in **Christ** will rise first."* (1 Thess. 4:16 NIV)

Out of all the nations on the earth, the Lord uniquely chose Israel to be His Wife. He gave her a written covenant of marriage at Mount Sinai. What Christians normally call "the Old Covenant" is a *Marriage* Covenant between God and Israel. The Lord's commitment to Israel is based on His covenants with Abraham, Isaac, and Jacob, and His commitment to the people of Israel at Mount Sinai. Because of the Patriarchs and the Covenants, He will never reject His chosen people. **The Lord gave Israel a New *Marriage* Covenant, and the Church has been grafted into the promises that were first given to Israel.** God is not finished with Israel and He is not finished with the Jewish people. We can trust the Lord to finish what He started. (Rom. 9-11)

CHAPTER 10:

The Wedding of the King's Son

The Great King of the Universe reminded me that our son's wedding was a living parable of the eternal union He has planned for His Son Jesus. Our son met his future wife while they both served the Lord as teenage missionaries. I had the great honor of officiating at their wedding. As the ceremony began, I stood at the front of the church with my Joe, and watched his beautiful, young bride approach. I thought about the wonderful Christian girl our son had chosen, and I understood that she was about to become a part of our family. I was then struck with further revelation concerning the scene playing out before me. My son's bride, in her pure white dress, became an earthly representation of the Lord's holy Bride. Just as I had dreamed my son would find a worthy bride to love him and make his life complete, our Heavenly Father has the same desire for Jesus.

I'm very grateful to God for our son and his wonderful bride. My pleasure over their marriage continues to this day, and they've now been married long enough to give us five beautiful grandchildren. **Jesus wants to have a Bride**, made up of people who are deeply in love with Him. His Father is incredibly overjoyed with the pending marriage of Jesus and His Bride. God is eagerly waiting for the day He can turn to Jesus and say, *"Son, the time for your wedding has come; go and* *get your Bride."* **We're called to be part of that Bridal Company.** Jesus knew all of this when He said:

Matt. 22:2 *"The kingdom of heaven is like a king who prepared a wedding banquet for his son."* NIV

In the verse above, Jesus presents foundational truth that really speaks to the entire purpose of Creation; the verse also gives us an interpretive key. Jesus said, *"The Kingdom of Heaven is like..."* He then goes on to describe what eternity is really all about. **The Kingdom of Heaven is about a King who prepared a wedding for His Son.** In this story, **God the Father is the *King*** and Jesus is *the King's Son.* The *"wedding banquet for his son"* speaks of **the mystic union of Christ and the Church.** The *"preparation"* that the Father has made is Creation itself and the redemptive story of Christ and mankind. God the Father began to plan the wedding of His Son before the foundation of the world. The *"wedding"* of His Son has been on His mind since time began. **Jesus is saying, *"If you want to understand the Kingdom of Heaven, the first thing you should know is that it's like a marriage between God and man."***

Marriage, in ancient Hebrew tradition, was initiated by the father of the groom.[50] Together with his wife, he would begin to determine what sort of woman would be best suited for their son. They would find a candidate that could be a worthy addition to their family and an asset for their son. The father would oversee and guide the entire process.

Just as a human father would have determined that it was time for his son to have a bride, in the fullness of time, God the Father determined that it was not good for His Son to be alone. The Lord decided that it was time for His Son to have a Bride that could join their eternal family and be worthy of Him. Jesus

---

[50] James M. Freeman, *Manners & Customs of the Bible* (New Kensington: Whitaker House, 1996), 26.

came into this world to redeem fallen mankind and make it possible for us to be with Him forever. God uniquely gave mankind free will, along with the ability to love Him and His Son Jesus. For the sake of His own great love, He made us candidates worthy to become His Bride. His revealed will all through the Bible, is to spend eternity with those who love Him. To convey this idea to us in a way we could understand, the Lord compared this relationship between Christ and the Church to a marriage.

Previously, I mentioned that Paul recognized this principle and expanded on it in Ephesians. Prophetically, **God created us to become one with Jesus, like a husband and wife do in a good marriage**.

> **Eph. 5:28** "*In this same way, husbands ought to love their wives as their own bodies. **He who loves his wife loves himself.** 29 After all, no one ever hated their own body, but they feed and care for their body, **just as Christ does the church**— 30 for **we are members of his body**. 31 'For this reason a man will leave his father and mother and be united to his wife, and the two will become **one flesh**.' 32 **This is a profound mystery** — but I am talking about **Christ and the church**.* NIV

The Kingdom of Heaven is all about God the Father preparing a wedding for Jesus. You were always intended to relate to God in a deep and profoundly intimate relationship. Perhaps for the first time, you've come to understand that you really don't know Jesus in this very personal way? The Lord is extending an invitation to you to come deeper. The Lord loves you, and I pray you'll respond to His love today. **You were created to be one with Jesus. The invitation is right before you; receive it now with great joy.** Take a moment to respond and thank Him for inviting you to become part of His Bride.

CHAPTER 11:

The Wedding At Cana

I n first-century Israel, most people lived in small towns and villages. These were places without organized sporting events or other regular community activities we now take for granted. Major religious festivals and weddings were the biggest entertainment average people had. To be invited to a wedding was an honor, and to be excluded could put you at risk of becoming a social outcast. Betrothals usually lasted about a year, so the upcoming wedding would be talked about for months, and then reminisced about for years afterward.

The actual wedding ceremony was followed by a celebration that normally lasted seven full days and nights. Along with the expected free food and wine, people would catch up on all the local and national news. In the days before newspapers, TV or the internet, news traveled by word of mouth. If you wanted to make a public announcement and be sure that it would spread far and wide, then a seven-day Jewish wedding was the place to do it.

The story of Jesus turning water into wine is well known, but the implications of the wedding setting are often overlooked. *Nelson's Bible Dictionary* correctly places an emphasis on Jesus attending the **Wedding at Cana** and choosing this setting for His first supernatural act. *"The significance of Jesus attending the marriage feast at Cana and performing His first miracle there can hardly be* *exaggerated.*"[51] The Bible gives us many parables, teachings and stories set in the context of weddings, to bring us a deeper revelation of the Bride of Christ. The story of the *Wedding at Cana* (John 2:1-11) is contained only in the Gospel of John.[52] **God chose this wedding as the setting to introduce Jesus as the miracle-working Messiah.**

There are no accidents in the Bible, and the Lord didn't accidentally choose a wedding for the scene of His public introduction to supernatural ministry. **The *Wedding at Cana* is the setting precisely chosen by God the Father, for the first public appearance and the first miracle of Jesus Christ.** John tells us that no miracle had ever occurred in the life of Christ prior to this, in clear contradiction to the *Koran* and false *Gospels* that claim otherwise. *"This, the first of his miraculous signs."* (John 2:11 NIV) **This first presentation of power, in the context of a wedding, prophetically revealed that Jesus' eternal ministry purpose is related to His ultimate wedding with the Church.**

The actual miraculous sign consisted of Jesus turning water into wine for the wedding feast. Jesus, several of his future disciples and Mary, His mother, were all gathered at a wedding in the city of Cana.

> **John 2:1** *"On **the third day a wedding took place at Cana** in Galilee. **Jesus' mother** was there, 2 and **Jesus and his disciples** had also been **invited to the wedding.**"* NIV

Mary approached Jesus and pled with Him to help the wedding party, because they had run out of wine. Jesus then instructed the servants to get six large pots or clay jars, fill them with water, and take them to the person overseeing the wedding celebration. *"Nearby stood six stone water jars, the kind **used***

---

[51] PC Study Bible, *Nelson's Illustrated Bible Dictionary* (CD-ROM, 2007), on "marriage."

[52] John 2:1 *On **the third day a wedding took place at Cana** in Galilee. Jesus' mother was there, 2 and **Jesus and his disciples** had also been **invited to the wedding.*** NIV

by the Jews for ceremonial washing, each holding from twenty to thirty gallons." (John 2:6 NIV) When it was tasted, the water had become better wine than what had been previously served.

The water pots or jars mentioned in this story were probably at the wedding to be used for purification of the various plates and other instruments, along with the religious washing of the hands of the guests and bridal party. Judaism later codified a highly developed system of ceremonial cleansing in the *Talmud* that was already in practice during this period.[53] There are many examples in the New Testament of the religious leaders rebuking Jesus for failing to uphold the traditional Jewish purification rituals.[54] Jesus took the six water pots that had been previously prepared for religious washing and turned them into vessels filled with wine for a joyous wedding feast. This breach of protocol would not have gone unnoticed by first century Jews.

The entire story shows the difference between true religion and false religion. False religion emphasizes rituals and regulations. **True religion celebrates an intimate relationship with Jesus.** The Bible teaches that Jesus came eating and drinking joyfully at a wedding. Jesus was holy, but not religious in the typical sense. Jesus was at liberty to turn religious ritual into a joyous wedding celebration, because God knew the ultimate plan of Heaven for His wedding with the Church. **God the Father chose this wedding miracle to reveal Jesus as Messiah, because a wedding is His ultimate destination and the very purpose for His human life and ministry.**

As a child, church attendance was mandatory for my entire family. My mother actually knew Jesus and related to Him in her daily life, but the rest of us just *"went to church."* In my childhood imagination, Christianity seemed to be about attending church, where they would present an endless list of compulsory

---

[53] David H. Stern, *Jewish New Testament Commentary* (Clarkesville: Jewish New Testament Publications, 1992), 164.

[54] See Matt 15:1-20, Luke 11:37-41 or Mark 7:1-15 for examples.

requirements that had to be carefully obeyed. Even as a child, I always believed in God, but I never dreamed that Jesus actually wanted to interact with me. Our Church presented no grid for knowing Jesus in a continuous cycle of ever-growing relationship. To me, He was portrayed as distant and formal.

The early disciples were expecting the Messiah to bring reform to their traditional religion, and governmental freedom from Rome. What they got was a loving Bridegroom who pledged, *"I will be with you always."* (Matt. 28:20 CJB) Jesus came to earth seeking a Bride who would be capable of returning His love. Right from the start, the Lord wanted us to know He would not be content with what had previously been acceptable. Jesus wants to share our lives, so that we might get to know each other as we enjoy life together. (John 10:10)

The supernatural, new life that Jesus brings is all-consuming, and our relationship with Him should never be consigned exclusively to weekly church meetings. You were born to know Jesus and be known by Him. He loves you, and He's extending His hand to you for regular fellowship. The relationship He desires, surpasses the capacity of meetings. If you will respond, He will merge His life with yours, and together you'll go progressively deeper into a life without end. You must transcend formal, religious tradition and move into loving intimacy with Jesus. Once you do, you'll never be the same.

CHAPTER 12:

John the Baptist

I was **baptized on October 3, 1971,** and Mary and I were **married on October 3, 1981.** This was not an intentional thing, and had I known the correlation, I would not have understood the significance. When we set our wedding date, I didn't know the actual date of my baptism. Twenty years after our wedding, I became the Pastor of the church where I had been baptized and discovered this interesting matching of dates while going through old records. God foreknew and foreordained that I would be baptized and married on the exact same date, ten years apart. There is prophetic significance in this *"coincidence,"* for my role in the Bride of Christ. **Water baptism and marriage are intertwined in the wedding customs of Israel.**

John the Baptist did not invent the Jewish custom of ritual immersion in water. In Judaism, a *"mikvah"* is a pool of water used for the purpose of ritual purification, and *"tevilah"* is the process of immersion in a *mikvah*. Sacred cleansing and immersion were used in Israel from the earliest times **to demonstrate repentance** and signify holiness before God. John built on this existing custom by calling the Jewish people to repentance and *tevilah* in preparation for their coming Messiah. The *New Unger's Bible Dictionary* tells us,

"The baptism of John was not Christian, but Jewish. It was, however, especially a baptism 'for repentance.' The only faith that it expressed concerning Christ was that His coming was close at hand. Those who confessed and repented of their sins and were baptized by John were thus obedient to his call to 'make ready the way of the Lord' (Matt. 3:3)."[55]

Some Christian traditions include forms of Baptism other than total immersion, but **all Christians baptize in water.** Water Baptism is a commandment that's a major part of every conversion to Jesus Christ, and it is connected to many things in the *New Covenant.* Baptism is the place of burial for our old Adamic nature, and it identifies us with the death, burial and resurrection of Jesus.[56] It publicly distinguishes us as members of the Church of Jesus Christ, and it speaks of the New Covenant Circumcision.[57] **Baptism also speaks to our preparation as part of the Bride of Christ.**

In modern Israel, it is required by law that all brides-to-be visit the *mikveh* in the week prior to their wedding.[58] From the time of Moses until this day, a bride must undergo *tevilah* in a *mikveh* before a marriage can be consummated. Some believe that immersion in the *mikveh* is even more important spiritually, than the

---

[55] PC Study Bible, *Unger's Bible Dictionary* (CD-ROM, 2007), on "baptism."

[56] Rom. 6:3-5 *Know ye not, that so many of us as were baptized into Jesus Christ were **baptized into his death?** Therefore, we are **buried with him by baptism into death:** that like as Christ was raised up from the dead by the glory of the Father, even so we also should walk in newness of life. For if **we have been planted together in the likeness of his death, we shall be also in the likeness of his resurrection.** KJV*

[57] Col. 2:11-12 *In whom also **ye are circumcised with the circumcision made without hands,** in putting off the body of the sins of the flesh by the circumcision of Christ: **Buried with him in baptism,** wherein also **ye are risen** with him through the faith of the operation of God, who hath raised him from the dead. KJV*

[58] Gross, *Under the Wedding Canopy,* 63.

rest of the wedding ceremony combined. They consider this ritual to be symbolic of many things, including a rebirth, with the *mikveh* representing the womb.[59]

The Jewish scholar David Gross wrote, ***"In a sense, getting married is like being born again."*** After making that statement, his point was that the couple is starting a new life together, but the wording is incredibly prophetic in its implications for Christians.[60]

These concepts of rebirth in marriage sound similar to Jesus' words to Nicodemus in John 3:3, ***"Jesus declared,** 'I tell you the truth, no one can see the kingdom of God unless he is **born again.**'"*** This might also explain why He seemed surprised that Nicodemus could not follow what He was talking about, *"'You are Israel's teacher,' said Jesus, 'and do you not understand these things?'"* (John 3:10 NIV)

The rabbis teach that the bride and groom represent God and Israel at Mount Sinai. Some also teach that before the Torah was given at Sinai, all of the Israelites had to immerse in a *mikveh*, just as Jewish couples do today before their wedding.[61] Perhaps that mass bridal sanctification was part of what Rabbi Paul had in mind two thousand years ago, when speaking of the Hebrew people, he wrote, *"...they all passed through the sea. **They were all baptized** into Moses in the cloud and in the sea."* (1 Cor. 10:1b-2 NIV)

I previously mentioned that Adam and Eve, as the first husband and wife, play prominent roles in both Jewish and Christian understandings of marriage. They, in the story of Creation, represent many things to both groups. There are seven steps leading down into a *mikveh*, representing the six days of creation, plus the Sabbath, and there are seven leading up, pointing to the re-creation of the person emerging from the pool. The purified person comes up as a new creation. God created man in His own image, and Adam and Eve's marriage was

---

[59] Kaplan, *Made in Heaven*, 74-77.

[60] Gross, *Under the Wedding Canopy*, 42.

[61] Kaplan, *Made in Heaven*, 78.

the pinnacle of Creation; so every marriage points back to the Lord's original plans for mankind.[62]

In addition to the marriage application, this same ritual act is required of converts to Judaism, just as baptism is required of new Christians. The Bible says that John's baptism was a baptism of repentance (Acts 19:4), but clearly the early Jewish believers also would have connected John's water baptism with rebirth and *"conversion."* John the Baptist spoke of **Christ** as the Bridegroom and said *"the **bride** belongs to the **bridegroom**."* (John 3:29) He spoke these words while he was in the process of immersing repentant Jews in water. They would have understood that ritual immersion was somehow connected with the concept of holiness and marriage. They must have marveled at John's words in **connecting baptism and the Messiah with a bride and a bridegroom.**

John the Baptist was asked if he was the Messiah, and he responded by **pointing to Jesus** with the words contained in the verse below.

> **John 3:29** *"The **bride** belongs to the **bridegroom**. The friend who attends the **bridegroom** waits and listens for him, and is full of joy when he hears the **bridegroom's** voice. That joy is mine, and it is now complete."* NIV

He explained that he was not the Messiah and went on to say that the Messiah was *"the Bridegroom."* John knew that his job was to prepare the way of the Lord by telling people they must repent and become holy so they could enter into a New *Marriage* Covenant with the Lord. John had seen Jesus and understood that his role was to act as His agent. He explained that he had been given the honor of serving as the human *Friend of the Bridegroom* in proclaiming that Jesus was the coming Bridegroom. **He understood that Jesus was the Messiah**

---

[62] Eisenberg, *The JPS Guide*, 555-557.

and Jesus alone is the Bridegroom. It was enough for John to know that the Bridegroom had now come and he had heard His voice.

Part of the wedding custom and preparation for every bride, was that she would undergo ceremonial immersion before the ultimate day of her marriage. This was also an established practice for **grooms** during their espousal period.[63] The practice of the bridegroom being immersed before his wedding day, may have been the custom Jesus alluded to when John first objected to His request for water baptism. *"Jesus replied, 'Let it be so now; it is proper for us to do this to fulfill all righteousness.' Then John consented."* (Matt. 3:15 NIV)

Jesus was baptized and became our Bridegroom. Every person who would become part of the Bridal Company must first be baptized in water. Water baptism is much more than an outward expression of an inward work. Water baptism separates us from the father of this world and prepares us for our marriage to Christ in the next. Each member of the Bridal Company must submit to being baptized during our days of preparation as the Bride of Christ. As a pastor, I often baptize new believers by immersing them in water. I always try to explain the Jewish Marriage custom of ritual immersion and connect their baptism to their mystic union with Christ.

The devil knows the written Word of God far better than any Bible scholar who ever lived, but he does not submit to what he knows. You can have knowledge without being born again or submitted to Christ. The Bride of Christ is saved, washed and made *"holy by the power of His Word."* (Eph. 5:26 CEV) Time spent reading the Bible is never wasted. Sanctification is a process that requires Bible study and obedience. Jesus is the Word made flesh. (John 1:14) We become part of the Bridal Company when we come to know Jesus as our personal Lord and Savior and continually submit to the washing of His Word.

---

[63] Arnold G. Fruchtenbaum, *The Footsteps of the Messiah* (San Antonio: Ariel Press, 2004), 160.

I want to conclude this chapter by reminding you of where we began. I was **baptized on October 3, 1971,** and Mary and I were **married on October 3, 1981.** The two events seemed unrelated, but they both had tremendous significance. Water baptism and marriage are intertwined in the wedding customs of Israel. As we have previously established, marriage is a parable of our relationship with Jesus. (Eph. 5:32) Through baptism, we were purified and prepared to join our eternal Bridegroom. Your baptism was part of the Biblical process that sanctified you for His Bridal Company. **You emerged from the waters of baptism as a new creation in Christ, and, together with the saved of all ages, you were joined to Jesus.**

CHAPTER 13:

The Dressing Room for Eternity

"This life is a dressing room for eternity, that's all it is."
Leonard Ravenhill

The New Testament invites us to see ourselves as the Bride of Christ, but it also portrays us in **different roles related to weddings.** In John 3:29 we can see ourselves in the role of *the Friend of the Bridegroom* explaining the virtues of Jesus to those who don't know Him. In the parable of the *Wise and Foolish Virgins* in Matthew 25, we are found as members of the wedding party who must consider if we are ready for the Bridegroom's arrival. We are called the *Children of the Bridechamber* in Matthew 9:15 (KJV) in speaking about fasting. In addition to all of those roles, we are *Guests Invited to the Lord's Wedding* in Revelation 19:9 and Matthew 22. These all apply to each of us in different ways. **Many different images are presented in a wedding context to convey different spiritual truths about our relationship with Jesus.**

When Jesus gave the parable of *the Marriage of the King's Son* in Matthew 22, He was speaking to a group of the chief priests and Pharisees, and they knew He was rebuking them. He began by saying, *"The Kingdom of Heaven is like a king who prepared a wedding banquet for his son."* The king had invited guests to his son's wedding, and they had refused to come. They gave many excuses, but none would have been considered valid. A wedding was often used in first century rabbinic parables, with God portrayed as a great king, and Israel as the king's son.[64] The Jewish religious leaders knew that Jesus was saying the Great King stood for God, but this time the people of Israel were being portrayed as the invited, but unwilling, wedding guests. They also would have understood that Jesus was presenting Himself as the King's Son.

I want to encourage you to read **Matthew 22:1-14** now, before we proceed further. Here is a brief recap of the important details contained in the parable:

The Kingdom of Heaven is about a Wedding.

The Wedding is for the Son of a King/God.

Jesus was declaring Himself to be the King's Son and our Messiah.

The Bride of Christ is *NOT* the focus of the story.

Believers are represented as *Guests* who have been invited to the Wedding.

Every Guest will be closely examined to see if they have proper *"Wedding Garments."*

The main point was that God had sent many servants (*prophets, faithful believers, etc.*) to invite the people of Israel to the Marriage of His Son Jesus, but the religious leaders had not let them come. Since His original guests were unwilling, the King had opened up the Wedding to all nations. Jesus used this parable to explain that the Jewish people (and all people) had been invited to the Wedding of the Son of God, and most had foolishly refused to come. Almighty God had invited them, and for anyone to refuse was a great insult. Israel was invited first, but now all mankind has been extended the invitation.

---

[64] Craig S. Keener, *The IVP Bible Background Commentary on the New Testament* (Downers Grove: Intervarsity Press, 1993), 104.

This story has also been called, *"The Man with No Wedding Garments,"* because one of the wedding guests showed up without proper attire. *"But when the king came in to see the guests, he noticed a man there who was not wearing wedding clothes. 'Friend,' he asked, 'how did you get in here without wedding clothes?'"* (Matt. 22:11-12 NIV) His point was that some would later respond to the invitation and come to the Wedding, only to find that they were not clothed in the proper wedding garments; **meaning, some who consider themselves as believers, will actually come to eternity and discover that they are not prepared for what is about to take place.**

The parable of *The Man with No Wedding Garments* clearly teaches that anyone who arrives in eternity at the Wedding Supper of the Lamb without the proper wedding garments, will not be allowed to participate in the Marriage celebration. The wedding garments are symbolic of our spiritual condition and not to be understood as literal clothing. **This spiritual attire is applied to us in our role as the invited wedding guests.** We are speaking of spiritual garments that can come only from living our lives for Christ. If you want to go to the Marriage of the Lamb, you must first be clothed in the proper attire. In this world we can fool each other as to our true spiritual appearance, but it will be obvious to everyone in eternity.

This consideration of having proper spiritual attire is not just a fringe illustration. There are many spiritual garments alluded to in the Bible, some that are good and some that aren't good. The Psalms tell us that we can be **clothed with cursing and violence.**[65] The Bible teaches that the ungodly will be **clothed with shame.**[66] The book of James tells us that improper use of riches

---

[65] Ps. 109:18 *As he **clothed himself with cursing** like as with his garment, so let it come into his bowels like water, and like oil into his bones.* And Ps. 73:6 *Therefore **pride** compasseth them about as a chain; **violence** covereth them as a **garment.*** KJV

[66] Ps. 132:18 ***His enemies will I clothe with shame:*** *but upon himself shall his crown flourish.* KJV

can **cause our spiritual garments to be ruined**.[67] We learn in Zechariah that **our spiritual garments can get filthy**, due to sinful behavior.[68] The book of Revelation speaks of those who have **defiled their garments** versus those who have *"overcome"* and walk with Jesus clothed in **white garments**.[69] In speaking to the church at Laodicea, Jesus tells them that they think everything is fine in their relationship with Him, but actually they are spiritually **naked**.[70]

We can become properly attired only by living in agreement with the Word of God. **Garments of Salvation** are mentioned in Isaiah 61:10, 2 Chronicles 6:41 and Psalm 132:16. Salvation is freely given by the Lord to true followers of Jesus. It requires only acceptance on the part of the recipient, because salvation is a free gift. **Other garments are connected to specific virtuous behavior.** I believe that the Bible presents these garments to explain spiritual principles. **They all speak of our walk with the Lord,** and although we cannot see them, it is quite apparent to the Lord if we have them or not.

In Revelation 16, Jesus revisits the theme of the *"The Man with No Wedding Garments."* He points to His second coming, saying it will be sudden, *"like a thief,"* and those who are awake and ready with their *"clothes"* are blessed people. *"Behold, I come like a thief!* **Blessed is he who** *stays awake and* **keeps his clothes with him,** *so that* **he may not go naked and be shamefully exposed.***"* (Rev. 16:15

---

[67] James 5:1 *Go to now,* **ye rich men,** *weep and howl for your miseries that shall come upon you. 2 Your riches are corrupted, and your* **garments are motheaten.** KJV

[68] Zech. 3:3 *Now Joshua was dressed in* **filthy clothes** *as he stood before the angel. 4 The angel said to those who were standing before him,* **Take off his filthy clothes.**" NIV

[69] Rev. 3:4 *Thou hast a few names even in Sardis which* **have not defiled their garments; and they shall walk with me in white:** *for they are worthy. 5 He that overcometh, the same shall be* **clothed in white raiment;** *and I will not blot out his name out of the book of life, but I will confess his name before my Father, and before his angels.* KJV

[70] Rev. 3:17 *Because thou sayest, I am rich, and increased with goods, and have need of nothing; and knowest not that thou art wretched, and miserable, and poor, and blind, and* **naked:** *18 I counsel thee to buy of me gold tried in the fire, that thou mayest be rich; and* **white raiment, that thou mayest be clothed, and that the shame of thy nakedness do not appear;** *and anoint thine eyes with eyesalve, that thou mayest see.* KJV

NIV) Revelation also indicates that **some garments must be washed.** It specifically says, *"blessed are those who wash their garments,"* because they can then enter the City of New Jerusalem and eat from the Tree of Eternal Life.[71] **White robes** are given to those who have been martyred for Christ,[72] and John also sees an immeasurable multitude, made up of every tribe, tongue and nation, before the throne of God dressed in **white robes.**[73]

The Lord has Bridal imagery woven all through the various garments mentioned in Scripture. **Here is a partial list of the spiritual garments:**

Garments of Praise	Is. 61:3
Garments of Salvation	Is. 61:10, 2 Chron. 6:41, Ps. 132:16
Garments of Vengeance	Is. 59:17, Is. 63:1-4
Rich Garments	Zech. 3:4
Garments Stained in Blood	Is. 63:2-3, Rev. 19:13
Clothing of Wrought Gold	Ps. 45:13
Raiment of Needlework	Ps. 45:14
Robe of Justice	Job 29:14
Robe of Righteousness	Is 61:10, Ps. 132:9, Job 29:14, Rev. 19:8
Robe of Splendor	Is. 63:1
Robe Dipped in Blood	Rev. 19:13, Is. 63:1-3
White Robe of a Martyr	Rev. 6:9-11
White Robe Washed in Blood	Rev 7:9-14, Rev 6:11, Rev 3:4

---

[71] Rev. 22:14 *"Blessed are those who **wash their robes**, that they may have the right to the tree of life and may go through the gates into the city."* NIV

[72] Rev. 6:11 *And **white robes** were given unto every one of them; and it was said unto them, that they should rest yet for a little season, until their fellowservants also and their brethren, that should be killed as they were, should be fulfilled.* KJV

[73] Rev. 7:9 *After this I beheld, and, lo, a great multitude, which no man could number, of all nations, and kindreds, and people, and tongues, stood before the throne, and before the Lamb, **clothed with white robes**, and palms in their hands.* KJV

Cloak of Zeal	Is 59:17
Turban of Justice	Job 29:14
Clean Turban	Zech 3:5
The Crown of Beauty	Is 61:3
The Crown of Splendor	Is 62:3
The Crown of Righteousness	2 Tim 4:8
The Crown of Life	James 1:12, Rev 2:10
The Crown of Glory	1 Pet. 5:4, Is. 28:5, Heb. 2:9, Ps. 8:5
The Crown of Honor	Ps. 8:5, Heb. 2:9
The Crown of Hope	1 Thess. 2:19
The Crown of Joy	1 Thess. 2:19
The Crown of Rejoicing	1 Thess. 2:19

Each of these items explain various ways that we as believers are being prepared for our eternal lives with Jesus.

The Bible clearly says that **Jesus is the foundation of our lives**, but it also speaks of spiritual *"silver, gold and costly stones,"* that we should use to build with during our lifetime.[74] These are **symbolic of the individual choices** that make up a life well-lived for Christ. Things done in agreement with the Word of God are compared to *"silver, gold and costly stones."* Examples could include Bible study, time spent in prayer, sharing the Gospel, etc. Conversely, poor choices are compared to worthless *"wood, hay and straw."* The Bible goes on to say that the Lord will *"test the quality of each man's work."* This means that my

---

[74] 1 Cor. 3:10 *But **each one should be careful how he builds**. 11 **For no one can lay any foundation other than** the one already laid, which is **Jesus Christ**. 12 If any man builds on this foundation using **gold, silver, costly stones**, wood, hay or straw, 13 **his work will be shown for what it is**, because the Day will bring it to light. It will be revealed with fire, and **the fire will test the quality of each man's work**. 14 If what he has built survives, he will receive his reward.* NIV

life will be examined to see if I have lived for the Lord or if all of my lifetime of *"works"* was focused on pleasing myself.

From the day we are born again, we begin to prepare for our eternal lives with Jesus. The garments we are given and the parts of our lives that have been built on Christ with spiritual **silver, gold and costly stones, all reflect the choices we make.** Every reward the Lord gives us, along with the things of eternal value produced by building our lives on Christ, **are the only things that go with us into infinity.**

In the world to come, all of eternity will know how we spent our lives, by viewing our spiritual attire. Perhaps even now, the angels and demons can see how we're really *"dressed,"* indicating the true depth of our walk with the Lord. Some, who we think of as being spiritual generals, may be dressed as new recruits or even as unbelievers. Or, their once spotless garments may have become stained from sin and willful disobedience. As the reader can see, spiritual garments are significant to the Lord, and I believe we wear them, even now.

God has prepared the means for each of us to be dressed and ready for the Marriage Supper of the Lamb. He has many spiritual items for us, consisting of all the Christ-centered choices we've made and the *"good works"* we've done during our lifetime. Our responsibility is to yield to His guidance, do the things He has prepared for us to do, and become the people He has called us to become. This does not mean that the Christian who works the hardest and gets the most accomplished wins.

My friend, the late Wade Taylor, loved to point out that the Lord says *"Well done"* to the good and faithful servants, not *"Much done."*[75] Our actions and choices are *"well done"* when they are led by His Holy Spirit, not measured by

---

[75] Matt. 25:21 *"His master replied, 'Well done, good and faithful servant! You have been faithful with a few things; I will put you in charge of many things. Come and share your master's happiness!'"* NIV

how much Christian activity we are involved in. If we live by His guidance, we will be among the invited Wedding Guests who are properly attired.

At some point in their lives, most people have dreamed that they were naked or not properly dressed in public. I've had those dreams, and perhaps you have too. This is a very common psychological manifestation, indicating we may have feelings of not being ready for something or that we feel inadequate for a situation. This type of dream may also be the Lord speaking to us about the true state of our relationship with Jesus. You and I can be ***spiritually naked.*** This is something the Lord is obviously concerned about.

In 1971, there was a day when I first responded to the Great King's Wedding invitation. I did this by accepting Jesus as my Lord and Savior. After I responded favorably, I walked away from God for a season and did not initially choose actions that would prepare me for my life with Christ. Years later, I made a decision to change my course of action, and I began to live in ways that will prepare me with proper wedding garments. In the years that have followed, I have tried to build my life on Jesus. I thank God for giving me a second chance, and because of His grace, I trust that I am not as spiritually naked as I once was.

One day soon, our lives will be over, and we will give an account of how we spent our days on earth. After reading the material above, you may be wondering what you are wearing in the Spirit and what you have to show for your walk with Him. I have good news for you! It is not too late to submit your life to the Lordship of Christ and the preparation of His Holy Spirit. The Lord has a list of every invited guest who accepts His invitation. This RSVP list is called the *Lamb's Book of Life.* (Rev. 21:27) **Ultimately, God will judge the invited guests who refuse to come. He will also decide who is properly dressed for the Wedding day, having spent their lives in preparation for *the Marriage of the Great King's Son.***

CHAPTER 14:

The Bride Made Ready

When Mary and I got married, her mother made her wedding dress. She and her Mom had found a beautiful dress in a magazine, and her mother was able to actually duplicate it from a pattern. It was full-length, shapely and voluminous in circumference at the bottom. The sleeves were semi-transparent, with sort of lacy-looking flowers woven in. There was a fancy matching hat, that had amazing slopes and textures on the wide brim. Honestly, the dress was extraordinary because it contained my beautiful bride on our wedding day. I keep a picture of her wearing that dress, on the wall of my office.

The Bible says a day will come when we need to rejoice, because the Bride of Christ will have, *"MADE HERSELF READY."* This will be the time for the Lamb's Wedding.

> **Rev. 19:7** *"Let us rejoice and be glad and give him glory! For **the wedding of the Lamb** has come, and **his bride has made herself ready**. 8 **Fine linen**, bright and clean, was given her to wear. **Fine linen** stands for the **righteous acts of the saints**."* NIV

Certainly when Revelation was written, John knew that the Bride's Price of salvation had been paid by Jesus at the Cross. But Scripture says, *"his bride has made herself ready."* Even though they were **saved by grace through faith in Jesus**, the Bride of Christ was somehow still responsible for her own spiritual preparation. **If they were saved, what was still needed?**

In ancient Israel, the espoused bride was expected to prepare her own wedding garments. She would also gather and prepare personal items that would be needed for her new life with her husband. She was supposed to be working diligently at this while the bridegroom was away preparing a place for them to live at his father's house.

The typical period between betrothal and consummation of the marriage was at least one year. The espoused and waiting bride was expected to diligently make the traditional marriage preparations. From time to time, reports would go back to the father of her intended husband, who would monitor her progress. Over this long period of separation, the bride would be tested for her faithfulness and her ability to function after the ultimate wedding.[76]

There were many things to be done, and some of these bridal customs have mystic implications for the Bride of Christ. The bride's **wedding garments** would traditionally be made of **fine linen.** Alluding to this marriage tradition, the Lord says that He (*the Husband*) gave Israel (*His Wife*) *"fine linen,"* in Ezekiel 16:10. Fine linen is mentioned 105 times in our Bible, and it appears in many Old Testament references to the Tabernacle of Moses and the garments worn by the Lord's priests. The fine linen symbolizes holiness, righteousness and virtue. It is a major component of the priestly garments.

Jewish bridegrooms would also wear **fine linen** in their wedding garments. Some Orthodox men still wear a linen garment for their wedding, known as

---

[76] Fruchtenbaum, *Footsteps*, 160-161.

a *"kitel,"* to symbolically represent the priestly garments.[77] They are normally made of white linen, which points to forgiveness, and in Jewish traditions it demonstrates that the bride and groom's sins are forgiven on their wedding day.[78] Some Orthodox men also wear a *kitel* on *Yom Kippur,* the Day of Atonement.[79] They do this because the white linen garment is reminiscent of the High Priest who wore one when entering the Holy of Holies, which some also equate to a Wedding Chamber. That connection with the Holy of Holies and forgiveness is why *huppahs* are normally made out of white linen. [80]

Fine linen is Biblically significant to the Bride of Christ. As our High Priest, **Jesus was wrapped in linen** at His burial.[81] Revelation 19:7 tells us there will be a day in the future when *"his bride has made herself ready,"* and she'll be given *"fine linen"* to wear. The implication is that the Bride of Christ is not yet fully prepared and ready to have Jesus return for His wedding. The writer connects the state of the Bride's readiness to the *"fine linen"* she's been given to wear.

Rev. 19:8 *"'Fine linen, bright and clean, was given her to wear.'*
*(Fine linen stands for the **righteous acts of the saints.**)"* NIV

He went on to explain that *fine linen* represents the *"righteous acts of the saints."* How were these things *"given,"* assumedly by God, and yet the Bride must do something called *"righteous acts"* to get them? It seems a little contradictory to say the fine linen is *given* to us, and yet we must do *"righteous acts"* to *get it.*

---

[77] Morlock, *Jewish Faith,* 101.

[78] Lamm, *The Jewish Way,* 186-187.

[79] Gross, *Under the Wedding Canopy,* 28.

[80] Kaplan, *Made in Heaven,* 151.

[81] Matt. 27:59 *And when Joseph had taken the body, he wrapped it in a **clean linen** cloth.* KJV

A partial explanation is given in Ephesians 2:10, *"For we are God's work-manship, created in Christ Jesus to do good works, which God prepared in advance for us to do."* This means that God has prepared *"good works"* that can be accomplished through your life, if you're willing. These are not just *"good works"* they are *"God Works."* These *"God Works"* are the *fine linen* or *righteous acts* that become the spiritual Wedding Dress for each of us as part of the Bride of Christ.

The Bride's righteous behavior has somehow allowed God to provide Her with otherworldly *fine linen.* It is easy to see that John was telling us our righteous behavior (*Godly actions*) prepares us to become part of the Bride of Christ. The Bridal Company that Jesus returns for will be those who have prepared their own wedding garments by acting righteously in accordance with the Word of God.

Scripture teaches that *"the righteous acts of the saints,"* provide us with spiritual *"fine linen"* that prepares us for our Wedding with Christ. Many *individuals* have acquired this fine linen over the millennia, but God is waiting for an *entire Bridal Company* to embrace His plans. Much *fine linen* is available, but few Christians choose to spend their lives in the righteous acquisition of it. The Bridal Company will be made up of those who have worked together and allowed the Holy Spirit to guide them through much preparation and many righteous acts. **The Bride of Christ will collectively be dressed and ready for Jesus on her Wedding Day, because they have spent their lives serving Him.** As part of the Bride of Christ, we should have something to show for our days on earth. In this case, it's represented as *fine linen.*

You are God's workmanship, but you have a part to play in that process. He will not form us into a holy Bridal Company unless we allow Him to. We must leave our old ways and prepare for eternity by learning His ways. Even as a Christian, you have the free will to **not** serve the Lord in individual situations. You must consciously yield to the will of the Holy Spirit for Him to do righteous

God Works through you. By saying *"yes"* to the Lord and doing His will, you are being **made ready** to function in His Kingdom.

Only those who are submitted and yielded to the Lord will be part of the Bride who has made Herself ready. **Jesus enables us to know Him, and He works through us. If that's what we desire, He will give us everything we need.** As we yield our lives to the purposes of God, we learn His ways and **we prepare ourselves** to dwell with Him forever. **His Bride will be ready** on the great day of the **Wedding of the Lamb**. May this be the generation of **His *Bride who has made Herself ready*.**

> **Rev. 19:7 *"'Let us rejoice and be glad and give him glory! For the wedding of the Lamb has come, and his bride has made herself ready. 8 Fine linen, bright and clean, was given her to wear.' (Fine linen stands for the righteous acts of the saints.)"* NIV**

CHAPTER 15:

The Bride Price

A few years ago, I was invited to attend a local wedding while I was on a mission trip in Liberia. After hours of preliminary formalities, music, and food, they started a VERY slow processional, bringing out an imposter dressed as the bride. A member of the bride's family then loudly began to ask the crowd to give him money to compensate the bride's family for the bride. There were many variations, but he basically said, *"how much will you pay us for our girl?"* He continuously explained how beautiful she was and how much her family loved her, while asking for more and more money. Almost everyone gave some money, including me. The assembled crowd would laughingly appease the barker with small amounts of cash until ultimately, they unveiled the bride and exposed her as an imposter. The fake bride was actually a small, veiled old lady! This continued with a series of four fake brides and four ransoms, until ultimately, they brought out the real bride.

Once the actual bride had been paid for, the real wedding service began. This entire process took several hours. They've made this tradition into a sort of interactive wedding theater. **I was told that in Liberia this is a standard part of every wedding.** The prospective groom's family is obligated to compensate the bride's family for the loss of their daughter, and they call this payment the

"Bride Price." People in many parts of Africa have variations on this practice of the groom's family paying a *Bride Price* to the bride's family.

In first century Israel, when a tentative agreement for marriage had been reached, the two families would get together and negotiate a payment that was also known as the *"Bride Price."* This was the price that had to be paid to her family by the groom's family to purchase or redeem her. The groom and his father would negotiate the bride's redemption price with the bride's family. **The amount of the *Bride Price* reflected the value or relative worth of the bride to the prospective bridegroom and his family.**

During Israel's early history, their economy was primarily agricultural. Domestic animals were often used to pay for the redemption of a bride from her family. A girl from a poor family might only bring a few small pigeons; whereas a more noble family might demand many valuable sheep and camels, or even precious gem stones. Sometimes the father of the bride would set a price and allow it to be worked off, as in the case of Jacob working seven years for his bride, Rachel. (Gen. 29) The more desirable the bride, the higher her family would set the Bride Price. If a high Bride Price was paid, it was a great compliment and constant reminder to the waiting bride of how much she was worth to her future husband.

As a result of original sin and our sinful nature, the Bible teaches that mankind became separated from God. We could never have become the Bride of Christ, because we belonged to this world and our father, the devil. (John 8:44) God found a way to purchase a Bride for His Son Jesus. **The Bride Price was the blood of our future Husband, Jesus Christ.** No higher Bride Price could ever be established than the mortal life of God's Son. (Heb. 9:15) Only by His sacrificial, atoning death, could the **Bride Price** for fallen man be paid in full and His Bride be redeemed. The price that was set reflected the value that God the Father and Jesus the Bridegroom, placed on the Bride. No higher price could have been established than the life-blood of Jesus, and no further payment for His Bride's redemption will ever be needed.

The writer of Hebrews tells us how Jesus actually felt when He was in the process of dying to pay the Bride Price, ***"Jesus, the author and perfecter of our faith, who for the joy set before him endured the cross."*** (Heb. 12:2b NIV) I often consider this verse when trying to understand **the price** that was **paid** for our *"free"* gift of **salvation**. Jesus somehow found the strength to endure the Cross, when He considered eternity spent with you and me. As the Owner and Creator of all things, Jesus was not looking for some reward in Heaven. By birthright, Jesus owns everything of value that has ever existed; except our love. (Col. 1:16-17) **You and I were the** *"joy set before him"* that helped Him somehow endure the pain of the Cross.

God the Father offered **Jesus** a Bride from among fallen mankind, fully understanding the Bride Price that would need to be paid. **Jesus** came to earth, knowing that His first role as our future Bridegroom would be to pay the Bride Price with His own sinless, mortal life. Neither the Romans nor the Jews took the life of **Jesus Christ**. He said, ***"No one can take my life from me. I sacrifice it voluntarily."*** (John 10:18a NLT) Our **Bridegroom gave His life willingly to pay the Bride Price for you and me.** We are the only Bride who was ever purchased by the Blood of our Bridegroom. **No higher price was ever paid, and no greater love has any man for his bride, than Jesus has for us.**

Paul was an observant Jew, but the Corinthian church that he wrote to was made up of both Jews and Gentiles. He wrote to tell them that they had been *"bought with a price."*

1 Cor. 6:20 *"For ye are **bought with a price**: therefore glorify God in your body, and in your spirit, which are God's."* KJV

This wording would have come with duel meaning to Paul's readers. Culturally, he could have been speaking of **slaves** that had been *"bought with a price"* or **women** who had been *"purchased"* with the **Bride Price**. Either way,

Paul was telling the people that **they had been purchased by the sacrifice of Jesus Christ,** so they no longer had independent rule over their own lives.

Most Middle Eastern cultures during the first century, had the practice of a groom paying a Bride Price. The specific term Paul used in this verse, *"bought with a price"* was part of a larger Jewish expression. As soon as the Bride Price was paid, the redeemed and now waiting bride was referred to as, *"One Who is Bought with a Price."*[82] This was the specific term that was used to designate a betrothed woman (*arusah*), prior to her wedding. It was applied to a waiting bride whose future husband had **paid the Bride Price in full.** The *One Who Was Bought with a Price* knew that her wedding was assured, because her future husband had already made a substantial investment to redeem her.

From the time the actual **Bride Price was paid in full,** the young lady would be treated quite differently by the people of her community. She no longer was considered to be single or available. She was now recognized as a married woman, and she was called specifically by the name of her betrothed husband. She would interact primarily with married women or others who had been ***Bought with a Price.*** Her days were spent in active preparation for the coming wedding as she remained watchful and ready for the coming bridegroom.

After the Bride Price had been paid, the bride and groom would be officially *"betrothed"* or *"espoused."* When the New Testament was written, a Jewish marriage consisted of two separate acts: **a formal espousal,** followed later by **the nuptial ceremony.** The first part of the wedding is the *espousal.* The Hebrew word for espousal, *"kiddushin,"* literally means *"sanctify,"* indicating that the couple has been sanctified and set aside for each other in a sacred relationship.[83]

The second part of the wedding is the nuptials, which came much later in ancient times and was called *"nisuin."* The word *nisuin* is derived from a word

---

[82] Zola Levitt, *A Christian Love Story* (Unknown: Self-Published, 1978), 3.

[83] Lamm, *The Jewish Way*, 161.

that means *"to take"* or to *"lift."*[84] To this very day, there are two parts in a traditional Jewish wedding ceremony, although they are no longer separated by long periods of time, having been combined into one service in the Middle Ages.

In Israel's early history, *espousal* **was far more binding than engagement is for us.** To be *espoused* meant that the couple were legally set apart and committed to each other, but they had not yet been intimate. **Most people would have treated them as if they were already married.**[85] There were formal writings detailing the espousal, drawn up by the religious authorities and kept on file. This sacred relationship could only be dissolved by divorce or the death of one of the parties.[86] That's why in the following New Testament account of Joseph and Mary's *"espousal,"* Joseph already was called Mary's *"husband."*

> **Matt. 1:18** *"Now the birth of Jesus Christ was on this wise: When as his mother Mary was* **espoused** *to Joseph, before they came together, she was found with child of the Holy Ghost. 19 Because* **Joseph her husband** *was a righteous man and did not want to expose her to public disgrace, he had in mind to divorce her quietly."* KJV

The **One Who is Bought with a Price** would often take out the marriage contract/*ketubah* and review the terms of her union with her beloved. **The New Testament is your Marriage Covenant.** So, in the same manner, you should read it often and consider the terms of your union with **Jesus.** It clearly explains your duties and responsibilities, along with the Lord's obligations toward you. The Bible contains all instruction for how you are supposed to lead your life until the coming Marriage Supper of the Lamb. (Rev. 19:9) It also reveals God's

---

[84] Kaplan, *Made in Heaven,* 136.

[85] Edersheim, *Sketches,* 148.

[86] Eisenberg, *The JPS Guide,* 31-33.

personality, His likes, His dislikes, etc., and in reading it we come to know Him better. It reveals details about our relationship and our eternal future together. **The Bible was given to those *Who Are Bought with a Price,* as a love letter.**

Paul said that you should honor God and ***bring glory to Him in your body.*** *"For ye are **bought with a price:** therefore **glorify God in your body,** and in your spirit, which are God's."* (1 Cor. 6:20 KJV) He was reminding us that we are not free to engage in improper sexual behavior. Christians are not to indulge in any type of sexual activity outside of marriage. Sexual sin dishonors God, and it dishonors us. Our bodies should be used to bring glory to God, by giving expression to His desires. **Jesus has paid the Bride Price for us, and He expects us to bring Him honor.**

He was telling us that we are no longer the same people we were before we entered into a Marriage Covenant. Jesus paid the Bride Price for us, and everything about us changed. From the time we are born again, we are not our own. Our lives should be different from those who HAVE NOT been **bought with a price.** The places we go, the people we associate with, and the things we do should be different. We're not to forget our old friends, but those *Who Have Been Bought with a Price* should spend most of their free time with other Christians when they are not engaged in being salt and light to the lost. (Heb. 10:25)

I can't even imagine the emotions God experienced as the terms of our **Bride Price** were determined. He knew that His Son would need to give His life to redeem us. Only the magnificent love of our Lord could have compelled Him to pay such a price. The value He placed on His Bride can never be equaled. May we never forget the price Jesus paid, and may we live each day as *One Who is Bought with a Price.* **May His joy be complete, when Jesus comes for *YOU* as His waiting Bride.**

CHAPTER 16:

The Last Supper

Matt. 26:26 *"While they were eating, **Jesus took bread, gave thanks and broke it, and gave it to his disciples**, saying, 'Take and eat; **this is my body.'** 27 Then **he took the cup**, gave thanks and offered it to them, saying, '**Drink from it**, all of you. 28 **This is my blood of the covenant**, which is poured out for many for the forgiveness of sins. 29 I tell you, **I will not drink of this fruit of the vine from now on until that day when I drink it anew with you in my Father's kingdom.'"** NIV*

I have prayerfully approached every word of this book with a sense of awe. That's as it should be, considering the holiness of the subject; but some of it is more holy than the rest. **Nothing is more Holy than the Blood of Jesus and Communion.** What I'm about to share presents an additional aspect of Holy Communion, connecting it to Jesus as our Bridegroom. This is not intended to contradict or invalidate any other Christian tradition concerning Holy Communion. I humbly submit the following thoughts for your consideration, in the earnest hope that they'll make you love and appreciate Jesus even more.

There are several bridal traditions contained within the details of the *Last Supper*. The obvious one is the *Marriage Supper of the Lamb*. I believe that Christ's celebration of His Last Supper on earth speaks of our first meal in Heaven with Him. *"Then the angel said to me, 'Write: "Blessed are those who are invited to the wedding supper of the Lamb!"' And he added, 'These are the true words of God.'"* (Rev. 19:9 NIV) Jesus may have been speaking of this Heavenly Marriage Feast when He said He wouldn't take the cup again until *"I drink it anew with you in my Father's kingdom."*

Additionally, Jesus made a speech at the *Last Supper* concerning His Second Coming, using very concise language that was traditionally used by Jewish bridegrooms for their brides. After the terms of the Marriage Covenant were settled, the groom would say, *"I am going to go prepare a place for you and when it is ready I will return to get you and you will live with me as my wife."*[87] Jesus used this specific Bridal language in speaking symbolically of His future Second Coming after His pending death and departure into Heaven. These words were traditionally reserved for the groom's intimate promise to return for his waiting bride. The custom was not obscure and should have been very familiar to the disciples of Jesus.

After the speech was completed, the intended groom would build an addition on his father's house for himself and his new bride.[88] Jesus spoke of this practice at the *Last Supper*, *"In my Father's house are many rooms; if it were not so, I would have told you. I am going there to prepare a place for you."* (John 14:2 NIV) The process of building could take a long period of time, and only the father could approve its completion and say, *"go and get your bride."* In

---

[87] John 14:1 *"Do not let your hearts be troubled. Trust in God; trust also in me. 2 In my Father's house are many rooms; if it were not so, I would have told you. I am going there to prepare a place for you. 3 And if I go and prepare a place for you, I will come back and take you to be with me that you also may be where I am.* NIV

[88] Kent, *The Greatest Love Story*, 130-131.

saying that He was *"going there to prepare a place,"* Jesus was assuring all of us that great care would be taken to provide us a future dwelling prepared at *His Father's House.* I first learned of these Hebraic practices while watching an excellent archeological and anthropological teaching series about Israel, produced by Focus on the Family in 1996; but I've since found them referenced in many sources.[89]

Jesus always taught about Communion in the context of Passover. The *Last Supper* was a *Passover Seder*, which is understood to have prophetic significance for **Jesus as the Lamb of God.** There are four long-established cups of wine used at Passover, with the last one known in some traditions as the *Cup of Acceptance.* **This cup signifies God's acceptance of His people.** The *Cup of Acceptance* may have been the cup Jesus used to institute **Holy Communion at the** *Last Supper.*[90]

In Jewish wedding customs, there's also a cup of wine known as the *Cup of Acceptance.* When a marriage agreement *(ketubah)* had been formalized, it was presented in writing, and the two parties sealed it by sharing *"the Cup of Acceptance."* This cup signified that the terms had been established and were **acceptable** to all parties.[91] The first step was **drinking from the** *Cup of Acceptance* and the second was the actual payment of the *Bride Price.* The father of the groom would pass the cup of wine to his son. If the groom accepted the terms of the marriage *ketubah*, he took the cup and drank some of it, signifying **his acceptance.** Next, the cup was passed to the bride for **her acceptance.** All parties

---

[89] Ray Vander Laan, *That the World May Know*, VCR video series, Set 3, Lesson 14 on Jewish Marriage. (Colorado Springs: Focus on the Family, 1996), This video series was the springboard for Vander Laan's excellent and greatly expanded ministry, *That the World May Know.*

[90] Luke's Gospel speaks of Jesus using two different cups in Luke 22:17 and v.20. Some believe that Jesus used **the Cup of Acceptance;** some think it was **the Cup of Redemption,** and some think He used both to introduce Holy Communion. Both cups clearly speak of our *acceptance* **and our** *redemption* celebrated in Holy Communion.

[91] Levitt, *A Christian Love Story*, 2.

knew that the marriage contract was not in force until the ***Cup of Acceptance*** had been drunk by both parties and the Bride Price had been paid in full.

Zola Levitt tells us that Luke 22:20, recorded at the ***Last Supper***, speaks specifically of the Jewish wedding custom of the bride and groom **sealing the marriage covenant by sharing the *Cup of Acceptance*.**[92]

> **Luke 22:20** *"In the same way, after the supper (Passover) he (Jesus) **took the cup**, saying, 'This cup is the new (marriage) covenant in my blood, which is poured out for you.'"* NIV

Holy Communion speaks of our pledge to marry Christ and of His commitment to us. While it's clear that Jesus was saying much more than this, He also intended to reaffirm His Marriage Commitment to the Bride of Christ in the context of the *Last Supper*.

The Disciples of Christ may have made the connection with the **Cup of Acceptance** as they recalled other words of Jesus, where a *cup* was mentioned. In the Garden of Gethsemane Jesus prayed, *"O my Father, if **this cup** may not pass away from me, **except I drink it**, thy will be done."*[93] Later that same night, Peter, with a sword, tried to defend Jesus at His betrayal. *"Jesus commanded Peter, "Put your sword away! **Shall I not drink the cup the Father has given me?"**[94] Peter must have known afterward that Jesus was saying His Father had agreed to the

---

[92] Levitt, *A Christian Love Story*, 12-13.

[93] Matt 26:39 *And he went a little further, and fell on his face, and prayed, saying, **O my Father, if it be possible, let this cup pass from me:** nevertheless not as I will, but as thou wilt. 40 And he cometh unto the disciples, and findeth them asleep, and saith unto Peter, What, could ye not watch with me one hour? 41 Watch and pray, that ye enter not into temptation: the spirit indeed is willing, but the flesh is weak. 42 He went away again the second time, and prayed, saying, **O my Father, if this cup** may not pass away from me, **except I drink it**, thy will be done.* KJV

[94] John 18:11 *Then said Jesus unto Peter, Put up thy sword into the sheath: **the cup which my Father hath given me, shall I not drink it?*** KJV

terms of the Marriage Covenant and made them known to Him. **In *"drinking the cup,"* Jesus had accepted His death as the price that must be paid.**

God considered His covenant relationship with Israel to be like a marriage. The word *"covenant"* often appears in Scripture to remind them of their Marriage to the Lord. Jesus lived a sinless life and died a sacrificial death on the Cross to set us free from our sins. He also died to satisfy the terms of our first Marriage Covenant, so we could enter into the ***NEW COVENANT***. **Jesus paid His life** to satisfy the Bride Price, and by doing that, He initiated our New *Marriage* Covenant. **The last words of Jesus from the Cross** were, *"it is finished,"*[95] meaning that His obligations as our Bridegroom and *Kinsman-Redeemer* had been **paid in full.**

When Jesus took the cup of wine at the *Last Supper*, He said, *"This cup is **the new covenant in my blood**, which is poured out for you."* (Luke 22:20b) **His own precious Blood was the price He willingly paid to initiate the New Marriage Covenant with His Bride.** Only Jesus could pay the Price for fallen mankind. He paid it in full, and we enter into the New *Marriage* Covenant with Him when we simply agree that *IT IS FINISHED*. By taking the **Cup of**

---

[95] **Jesus drank wine that was *"sour,"* moments before He actually died on the Cross.** John 19:28 *Jesus, knowing that all was now finished (ended), said in fulfillment of the Scripture, I thirst. [Ps 69:21.] 29 A vessel (jar) full of **sour wine** (vinegar) was placed there, so they put a sponge soaked in the **sour wine** on [a stalk, reed of] hyssop, and held it to [His] mouth. 30 When Jesus had received the **sour wine**, He said, **It is finished!** And He bowed His head and gave up His spirit.* AMP By drinking the sour wine on the Cross, He signified once again that He willingly took the Cup of Acceptance, agreeing to the difficult (*sour*) terms of the marriage contract. **Jesus drank the *sour wine*, then uttered *"It is finished"* and died.** One Greek word is translated as the three English words, "*it is finished.*" The Greek word is "*teleo*" (tel-eh'-o) and it can mean much more than "*it is finished.*" **It means to complete a transaction or execute a contract. It also means to discharge a debt.** (For more complete details on "*teleo*" see #5055 in Strong's Greek Dictionary, Thayer's Greek Lexicon, the Louw and Nida Greek-English Lexicon and Vine's Expository Dictionary of NT Words.) When Jesus uttered this word, *teleo*, He meant to convey that **all of our debts were discharged and our marriage contract was completely valid. Jesus paid** the Bride Price with His life and **at that very moment, He put the New *Marriage* Covenant into force.**

Acceptance, Jesus committed to the payment of His life to redeem the Church, and by doing so, He **accepted you as part of His future Bride. All He requires in return is your love.**

At the *Last Supper*, **Jesus said this is the New Covenant** *"in His Blood."* A blood covenant implies that both parties are committed to each other, by life or by death. In like manner, when we take the cup at Holy Communion, we're not only acknowledging what Jesus did for us at the Cross, but we're affirming a similar level of devotion to Him. When Jesus took the *Cup of Acceptance*, it was symbolic of His willingness to give His life for us. When we take the cup in Communion, we're signifying that our obligation to Him is nothing less. The *Cup of Acceptance* **signifies** both His Marriage commitment to you and yours to Him. **When you take the cup in Holy Communion, always remember the price that Jesus paid as our Bridegroom, and always express your love and steadfast allegiance to Him.**

> **Phil. 1:20** *"I eagerly expect and hope that I will in no way be ashamed, but will have sufficient courage so that now as always Christ will be exalted in my body,* **whether by life or by death.** *21* **For to me, to live is Christ and to die is gain.**" NIV

CHAPTER 17:

Jesus Is Coming

A mong many Spirit-filled Christians in the late 1960s and early 1970s, there was a tremendous sense of anticipation for the Second Coming of Jesus Christ. With the return of Jerusalem to Jewish control for the first time in over two thousand years, Biblical prophecy was being fulfilled before our very eyes. The Charismatic Renewal and the Jesus People Movement were in full swing. Urgent exhortations and prophetic words were spoken at almost every meeting, declaring that the end of the world was near.

The church we attended in those days was fully invested in this expectation. We often prayed and sang songs reflecting our belief that the Second Coming of Jesus would be soon. Our Pastor included variations on this theme in most of his sermons. We heard regular accounts of people picking up mysterious angelic hitch-hikers who'd solemnly proclaim the soon coming of Jesus, then disappear. Ordinary conversations at the church were filled with various expressions of, *"Jesus is coming soon."* As a young teenager, I used to wonder if we were going to actually make it home from church before Jesus came! Sadly, that expectant mindset for the Second Coming of Christ is no longer widely accepted. It was intense and difficult to sustain, but it certainly kept us focused on Jesus.

The healthy expectation for the imminent return of Jesus for His Bride is a solid Biblical attitude. Several of the New Testament writers implied that they expected Christ to return in their own lifetimes. And Jesus Himself, spoke often about His return. He gave us several looks at the Second Coming with parables in the context of a wedding. This was His way of saying that He would be returning to claim the Bride of Christ.

The ***Parable of the Wise and Foolish Virgins*** in Matthew 25:1-13 is about the Second Coming of Jesus. He begins the parable with, *"Then the kingdom of heaven will be like,"* and then tells a story about ten virgins in a **wedding party,** who were supposed to go out and meet the **Bridegroom** for the actual wedding. They were aware that the wedding was supposed to be soon, but there was a long delay and when it was finally announced, they were surprised by the Bridegroom's sudden arrival. The ten virgins were supposed to each have an oil lamp for use in the wedding processional back to the Bridegroom's Father's house, but five didn't have any oil. Five of them were ready, and five were not ready. The five virgins who had enough oil to supply their burning lamps were called *"wise."* They got to attend the wedding, but the five *"foolish"* virgins ran out of oil and were excluded.

The entire parable is set in the context of a marriage. **Jesus is the Bridegroom and Christians** are portrayed as **the ten virgins** invited to the wedding. The story came as part of His description of what conditions will be like on earth when He returns. The *"oil"* represents **the Holy Spirit** and His anointing, given freely to prepared disciples of Christ. Opinions vary about the symbolic details, but the principal meaning is that **Christians must remain ready for the coming of the Lord, and some will NOT BE READY.**

Remember, **Jesus spoke these words as He was responding to a question about what it would be like when He returned to earth.** He replied with this parable about some who were ready and some who were not ready for a wedding. His objective was for all believers be ready for His coming, but He was clearly warning us that it was possible to be caught unprepared. He wanted us to know that a day will come when there's no more time for preparation. **His guidance was that we must live with a constant readiness for His Second Coming.**

The *Parable of the Wise and Foolish Virgins* was intended to create **an urgent expectation for the Second Coming of Christ.**

> **Matt. 25:6** *"At midnight the cry rang out: 'Here's the bridegroom! Come out to meet him!'"* NIV

This *"midnight cry"* was shocking in its suddenness, as was the invitation to *"Come out to meet Him;"* but these elements were part of the wedding traditions of the time. Weddings were often held at midnight to add the element of surprise.[96] The wedding party had to be ready and alert for the announcement at any time. When all wedding preparations had been finalized, the Bridegroom's Father would tell *the Friend of the Bridegroom* to announce the wedding. He would go throughout the community shouting these words, *"Here's the bridegroom! Come out to meet him!"* and he would continue to proclaim his good news until the groom actually arrived.[97] This would serve to notify the bride and invited guests that the day of the wedding was at hand.

Jesus directly presented Himself as *"the Bridegroom"* in connection with *the Midnight Cry*. I believe He had at least two intended points when He mentioned *"midnight."* First, He wanted us to know He will return at a time that may surprise us. On the same occasion that He gave us this parable, He said, *"you also must be ready, because the Son of Man will come at an hour when you do not expect him."* (Matt. 24:44 NIV) This speaks to our needing to remain spiritually alert at all times, so that we are not found unprepared. More importantly,

---

[96] Freeman, *Manners & Customs*, 376-379.

[97] Keener, *IVP Bible Background*, on Matthew 25:6.

I believe He used *"midnight,"* the common hour of a first century Jewish wedding, to say He will be returning for the Bride of Christ. **The return of Christ is all about the culmination of our divine romance.**

The *Midnight Cry* is the final proclamation of the return of the Lord. This will be a season of time, climaxing the Lord's plans for mankind. Those unprepared for His coming *(the foolish)* will unsuccessfully try to hide. (Rev. 6:15) The Bible clearly explains that Jesus is coming for His Wedding. He will come at His Father's direction to receive His Bride when all things have been made ready. The reader should consider that Jesus has been preparing a place for His Bride for almost 2,000 years. If all of the created order was made in seven days, then our future home must be quite a place. As believers, we **must always be ready for the imminent return of Jesus Christ and the Marriage Supper of the Lamb.**

Friends, we must live our lives with an urgent expectation that Jesus is coming soon. If we are wise, we'll live this way. He will come at a time when the world doesn't expect Him. It also will be a time that many Christians are no longer looking for Him. As the signs of His pending arrival intensify, we should let our wedding lamps shine ever brighter in proclaiming Jesus to this lost world. From what I see, He's soon to appear. His wise and waiting Bridal Company must be willing and ready to *meet Him when He comes.* **The end of this world will be the Wedding Day for the Bridal Company of Christ. Jesus is coming soon.** Be wise, and be ready.

1 Cor. 16:22-24 *"If anyone does not love the Lord, let him be separated from God — lost forever! Come, O Lord! The grace of the Lord Jesus be with you. My love be with all of you in Christ Jesus."* NCV

CHAPTER 18:

CONSIDER Our Bridegroom

I t is my firm belief that many genuine Christians have very little personal interaction with Jesus. It's imperative that we relate to Him as more than just an absentee owner of creation and the invisible deity who hears our meal-time prayers. The Bible says our relationship with Him should, in many ways, be like a good marriage. To be married to someone, you must know them well. It's time to know Jesus as He has really revealed Himself. **We must interact more with Jesus to actually know His personality. Many Christians are saved, but hardly know Him.**

In the year 2000, I heard a message that **John Arnott**, pastor of the Toronto Airport Fellowship, gave at a conference in Florida. He talked for about an hour, but the only thing I remember him saying is one phrase, *"God is the nicest person I ever met."* That completely messed with my thoughts on several levels, and I mentally shut down after he said it. I began to wonder, *"What on earth is he thinking?"*

My first idea was that he was being disrespectful to God by even calling Him a *"person."* It seemed to me, that he was in some way making God small and trying to bring Him down to our level by calling Him a *"person."* At the same time, I was stuck on his observation that not only was God a *"person,"* but he thought God was *"the nicest person he ever met."*

Whatever I thought of God at that point, I didn't think of Him as a person, and I certainly never would have described Him as being *"nice."* As a young believer, I served a God who was, in my mind, looking for an excuse to send each of us to hell. That thinking took me down some dark roads, but with the help of God, I had gotten past it over the years. Even though I'd come to know the Lord as loving and merciful, I still had a pretty standoffish view of God at the point I heard Pastor Arnott. A few of the adjectives I might have used to describe the Lord were, *"holy," "just," "merciful," "forgiving," "righteous," "almighty,"* etc., but I would've NEVER, EVER said He was *"nice."* After hearing Pastor Arnott, I was confronted with two possibilities; either John Arnott was a very mixed up man, or he knew the Lord in a way that I didn't. One of us was confused, and it turned out to be me!

I couldn't stop wondering if Pastor Arnott was right, so as I meditated on these things, I began to focus on the question, *"How could he say that God is a person?"* The philosopher John Locke defined *"person"* this way, *"A person is a thinking, intelligent being that has reason and reflection, and can consider itself as itself, the same thinking thing in different times and places."*[98] God is certainly a thinking and intelligent being. He has the ability to reason and reflect, etc.; so by Locke's definition, clearly **God is a *PERSON*.**

Next, I looked up *"personality."* The *Encarta World English Dictionary* defines *"personality"* as *"The totality of somebody's attitudes, interests, behavioral patterns, emotional responses, social roles, and other individual traits that endure over long periods of time."*[99] The Bible reveals God's *attitudes, interests,* etc. over a loooooooooong period of time, so that works too. Clearly, by these

---

[98] PC Study Bible, *Unger's Bible Dictionary* (CD-ROM, 2007), quoting John Locke on the definition of *"person."*

[99] *Encarta ®World English Dictionary*, Microsoft Word, on the definition of *"personality."*

definitions, **God is a *"person,"*** and God has a *"personality."* So, I began to consider the individuality of our Bridegroom, and I continue to meditate on that to
this very day. **Since we're going to spend eternity with Jesus,** I thought it was
important to get to know our **Bridegroom** a little better.

Once I saw these things, I asked myself another question, *"Can we actually
know Jesus as a real person?"* I made that question into a prayer, and the Lord
brought a verse to me that pointed me in the right direction. *"Jesus said unto him,
Thou shalt **love** the Lord thy God...**with all thy mind.** This is the first and great
commandment."* (Matt. 22:37-38 KJV) I knew about the *"love"* part and had
spent many years preaching on it, but the word *"mind"* jumped out at me. *Can
you love God with your mind?* To me, it suddenly seemed that the Holy Spirit
was saying God had given me a good mind as a tool that I could use in knowing
Him and seeking Him. So, I set my mind to do just that. I've now come to believe
that to truly know our GOD as the person He really is, we **must** apply our *minds*
to understand His personality.

This is complex, because we are talking about *the personality of God.* Most
people have some knowledge of His moral attributes and His divine nature, but
almost no mental picture of His personality. **Jesus is a lot like His Father.** They
freely interact, and sometimes it's difficult to determine where one leaves off
and another begins. Jesus explained this principle to Philip when he asked to
see God the Father:

> **John 14:8** *"Philip said, 'Lord, **show us the Father** and that will
> be enough for us.' 9 **Jesus answered: 'Don't you know me, Philip,**
> even after I have been among you such a long time? **Anyone who
> has seen me has seen the Father.'"*** NIV

Having gotten that far with my thinking, I began to study my Bible intensely
to determine what it says about His *personality.* He introduced Himself to

Moses in this way, *"The Lord, the Lord, the compassionate and gracious God, slow to anger, abounding in love and faithfulness, maintaining love to thousands, and forgiving wickedness, rebellion and sin."* (Ex. 34:6-7 NIV) He told Moses that He was, **"compassionate and gracious," "slow to anger, abounding in love and faithfulness, maintaining love to thousands."** To me, that seemed to be a little bit *"nicer"* than what He had previously revealed about Himself in parts of Genesis and Exodus.

I soon found that the LORD is a very passionate person, because to be "passionate" means to express strong emotions, and God has plenty of those. The LORD has a great sense of humor, because "humor" is the ability to enjoy or perceive what is amusing. (Ps. 2:4, Ps. 37:13) Of course, I figured out that the LORD is very creative. In fact, His creativity transcends all of the artists who have ever lived; *"In the beginning God **created**..."* (Gen. 1:1) I quickly found dozens of passages with details on what He likes and dislikes, but what I was starting to see was hard to define. In short, He was beginning to look like He might be the best of the best in anything virtuous I could think of. In other words, God originated *personality*, and He *exemplifies* each aspect to their highest degree. **He's the Greatest in every category.**

The LORD is a person, and He has a personality. Our God created us to have personalities much like His. (Gen. 1:27) Of course we see that in the Bible, but we also must spend time with Jesus to know Him as a person. All of these big thoughts and ideas about His *"personality"* must be discussed with the *"person"* we are trying to get to know; but I digress.

Over the last years, I began to keep notes on the traits I've found revealed in God's personality. My Biblical research now runs many, many pages, but here are a few of the things that Scripture reveals about the Lord's personality.

- The LORD is Passionate.   Isa. 42:13-14
- The LORD has a sense of Humor.   Ps. 2:4
- The LORD is Creative.   Gen. 1:1

- The LORD is full of great Joy.   Zeph. 3:17
- The LORD is Gentle and Humble.   Matt. 11:29
- The LORD is Compassionate.   Ps. 86:15
- The LORD is Fair and Impartial.   Deut. 10:17
- The LORD is Loyal.   Matt. 28:20
- The LORD is Patient.   2 Peter 3:9
- The LORD is Honest.   Titus 1:2
- The LORD is Faithful.   1 Cor. 1:9
- The LORD is pure Love.   1 John 4:16
- The LORD is Zealous.   Isa. 9:7
- The LORD is Forgiving.   1 John 1:9
- The LORD is Appreciative.   Matt. 10:42
- The LORD is Merciful.   Deut. 4:31
- The LORD is Kind.   Rom. 2:4
- The LORD is Peaceful.   Phil. 4:9
- The LORD is Wise.   Jude 25

Do you like people who sing and are full of great joy? God invented singing and joy; and God is a happy person, *"Cheer up, Zion! Don't be afraid! For the **LORD your God** has arrived to live among you. He is a mighty savior. **He will rejoice over you with great gladness. With his love, he will calm all your fears. He will exult over you by singing a happy song."** (Zeph. 3:16b-17 NLT) Do you love gentle people? The LORD is a gentle and humble person. *"Learn from me, for **I am gentle and humble in heart**, and you will find rest for your souls."* (Matt. 11:29b NIV)

As I have prayerfully considered this whole matter, here's the bottom line: **God invented every human virtue, and every decent characteristic we admire in others is a partial fulfillment of being** *"created in His image."* (Gen. 1:27) Any virtuous, Godly person we have high regard for (spouse, friend, grandparent, leader, etc.), is able to reflect only a small fraction of *HIS IMAGE*. The same wonderful attributes that we see in others, are found in God without measure. Every good thing we admire, God thought up and He demonstrates in His own life.

The Bible directly describes a lot about God's personality, and we dare not go in opposition to the revealed Word of God. However, Jesus also reveals Himself to us individually, as we interact with Him. One of my recurring prayers is, *"Jesus, I want to know You as well as a living man can."* In response to my desire, the Lord has revealed some surprising aspects of Himself through various means. One of the personal ways Jesus interacts with me is that He speaks to my heart concerning subjects that I'm not actually thinking about at that moment; or, thoughts that run contrary to my limited understanding of our limitless God. I've come to recognize many of these "thoughts" as the still, small voice of Jesus.

Example: One morning I was sitting at our kitchen table drinking coffee and listening to news on the radio. Since nobody was in the house, as I heard something particularly interesting, I'd comment on it out loud to the Lord. I wasn't praying exactly, and He wasn't saying anything back to me. I was just having a little fun commenting on what was being said, without really thinking about the implications. Suddenly, I caught myself as I realized these were *"secular"* current events that I was pointing out to God. Definitely inappropriate! Feeling a little silly and not very spiritual, I said, *"Hey Lord, I'll bet David never talked to You about stuff like this."* To my great surprise, the Lord responded immediately, **"You'd be surprised what David and I talked about."** I did NOT expect that! Those were not my natural thoughts. God was speaking to me.

That completely unexpected *"thought,"* *"You'd be surprised what David and I talked about,"* set my imagination on fire. Instantly I thought, **"David was a man after God's own heart. How did he get that way? What sort of things did they talk about?"** It certainly wasn't a matter of David just quoting a bunch of Bible verses to God! And **David probably didn't divide his interaction with the**

Lord into *"secular"* versus *"sacred,"* but... **I suddenly realized that I did.** That coffee-time encounter happened years ago, but it's still unfolding in my spirit.

On another occasion, I was with three friends on a covert mission trip in a closed country. It was illegal for us to minister there, and the police broke up our meetings and began to follow us. Our hosts were not intimidated, but we four Americans were a little frightened. To lessen the tension, I started making wise cracks about our situation and continued doing so for the rest of the trip. On the last day, one of my fellow countrymen said that my playful comments changed his perspective and really made the whole experience "fun." Immediately, **Jesus** spoke to me with another unexpected thought, ***"Why don't you ever talk to Me like that?"*** I was shocked. Can a living man speak playfully to God? Is God interested in hearing my ironic observations about life? **Friends, I now know that He wants us to talk to Him about every aspect of our lives.**

The Lord was stretching my understanding of His personality and inviting me to share more of my life with Him. He also was moving out of the church box I had constructed for Him. We serve a God who refuses to be systematized or limited. He's limitless. Now I talk to the Lord about many things; often out loud. Some are private things that I don't share with anyone else, but I also talk to Him about the everyday things I'd share with a good friend. I interact with the Lord about daily things and the simple irony of life. You should try this, because I think He likes it.

On and on it goes, but I hope you get the point. God has the most wonderful *"personality"* of any being who ever existed. Nobody can compare with Him. John Arnott was right; God is the nicest person that any of us ever met and will ever know. If you put together all the *"nice"* people who have ever lived, their combined *"niceness"* would not begin to equal God's. In fact, God is the best person there is in every good category that exists. To be with Him, is to be with the best. As part of the waiting Bridal Company of Christ, we need to really know Him as He wants to be known. Not only should we love Him, we should like Him as a person and admire Him, too. He is great to be with in all seasons, and He *"personifies"* every good thing there is.

John G. Lake said this, *"Men are afraid of God because of wrong concepts. Let a man meet God in Jesus, and he will love God."*[100] Someone else has said the problem is never with people not wanting Jesus; the problem is with people not wanting the Jesus most Christians present. In other words, the problem is not with God's real personality; the problem is that we don't know Him as He has really revealed Himself to be. All of our false concepts about God will someday drop away like so much dead grass when we die, but I want to encourage each of us to see Jesus as a person now. He knows that we will fall even deeper in love with Him when we know Him better. He loves us and wants to spend eternity with us, and I really sense that Jesus would be excited to reveal His personality as it actually is. Why don't you ask Him to show Himself to you in a fresh way? Jesus is the nicest person you will ever know, and He's waiting to hear from you.

---

[100]Unknown. *Heroes of the Faith (Tulsa: Harrison House, 1996),* 16.

CHAPTER 19:

CONSIDER His Bride

My wife and I started talking about going into full-time ministry years before we actually did it. I didn't know at the time, but Mary was going through a struggle that she didn't share with me. She was concerned that she could never be *"a good Pastor's wife."* In her mind, she'd be on display at all times, and she'd need to appear perfect to every outside observer. This was an impossible standard for anybody to live up to. One day, she met the very down-to-earth wife of a minister friend of mine. This lady was sweet and Godly, but not perfect. After interacting with her for a long weekend, Mary decided that if that woman could be a good Pastor's wife, she could too.

God has offered us a divine romance and preparation for eternity. Jesus is coming back for a Bride who wants to be with Him forever. **The Bride of Christ will be made up of normal people just like you.** Your preparation as part of the Bride begins when salvation occurs, and it's a process that may take a lifetime to complete. The preparation takes on many facets, but all of it is for ordinary people who love an extraordinary Savior.

Jesus explained that the Kingdom of Heaven is all about a Great King who made a Marriage Feast for His Son. God the Father is the Great King; Jesus is His Son; and the Marriage Feast is the eternal celebration that will be held between

Jesus and His redeemed Bridal Company when time is no more. The Bride is *"neither male nor female."* Jesus is not looking for the perfect WOMAN, and He's NOT looking for an opposite personality. **In this case, opposites do not attract.** His Bridal Company will be made up of saved people who've allowed the Holy Spirit to reshape their nature to look much like His. Everyone on Earth is invited, but few choose to accept.

Adam and Eve were the first married couple. They participated in Earth's first marriage, the most intimate relationship available to mankind. Paul explains that their marriage typifies the intended relationship between Jesus and His Bride. Together, Adam and Eve knew God and walked with God, INTIMATELY. They are the prototype for the Bridal Company of Christ in terms of our corporate relationship. We're called to love each other and love the Lord. We're supposed to walk with each other, while walking closely with the Lord. Like Adam and Eve, the Lord is supposed to be in the midst of our relationships with other Christians. The Bride of Christ is made up of those who have a heart for the Lord and a heart for other believers.

The Biblical imperative is for us to have a relationship with Jesus that's like a good marriage. This example is not only intended for married people. In the New Testament, John the Baptist never married, yet he identified Jesus as the *Bridegroom* and himself as the *Friend of the Bridegroom*. Paul never married, yet he revealed the connection between marriage and our relationship with Christ. As far as we know, John the Beloved Apostle never took a wife, but he revealed the Lord's Bride as the City of New Jerusalem. And Jesus Himself never married, but He often taught about the Bride of Christ and our relationship with Him. **Married or single, these truths are for you.**

Israel, as a nation, was married to God in the *"Wedding at Mount Sinai."* Millions of Jews were collectively wooed by Almighty God, and they entered into a *Marriage* Covenant. Israel as the national ***Wife of God*** is the prototype for the ***Bride of Christ***. Individual Jews didn't consider themselves to be the *"**Wife of***

God," but collectively as a nation, they were married to the Ancient of Days. In the same way, the true Church, as the *Bride of Christ,* is *married* to **Jesus.** The Bridal Company is made up of all redeemed individuals, both Old Testament and New Testament.

Abraham's servant told Rebekah all about Isaac, and in the same way, **the Holy Spirit teaches us all about Jesus.** Ruth's mother-in-law Naomi, instructed her in the customs of their people so she could attract Boaz for her husband. In like manner, the Holy Spirit teaches us about the ways and customs of the Lord. And, just like Mordecai and Hegai instructed Esther in the protocol of the Lion King, the Holy Spirit guides us in our preparation for marriage with Jesus. **It's the job of the Holy Spirit to show us what Jesus is looking for in a Wife.** All we must do is yield to His guidance and preparation. If you're a person who loves Jesus, you already qualify.

The *Personality of the Bride* is supposed to be similar to the *Personality of Jesus.* Most of the stuff He's looking for can be found concisely contained in one passage from Galatians. It all comes to us in seed form when we are born again, then grows as we mature in our faith. These characteristics are called the *"Fruit of the Holy Spirit."* Here is what the Amplified Bible says:

> **Gal. 5:22** *"But the fruit of the [Holy] Spirit [the work which His presence within accomplishes] is **love, joy** (gladness), **peace, patience** (an even temper, forbearance), **kindness, goodness** (benevolence), **faithfulness,** 23 **Gentleness** (meekness, humility), **self-control** (self-restraint, continence). Against such things there is no law [that can bring a charge]."* AMP

Jesus wants people who love Him, with natures similar to His. The observant reader will quickly see that **the Lord wants His Bride to have the same characteristics He reveals in Himself.**

- Love. **1 John 4:16** God is love.
- Joy. **Neh. 8:10b** For the joy of the Lord is your strength.
- Peace. **Isa. 9:6** The Prince of Peace.
- Patience. **2 Peter 3:9** He is patient with you.
- Kindness. **Jer. 9:24** I am the LORD who exercises kindness.
- Goodness. **Ps. 34:8** Taste and see that the LORD is good.
- Faithfulness. **2 Thess. 3:3** But the Lord is faithful.
- Gentleness. **Matt. 11:29** I am gentle.
- Self-control. **Ex. 34:6** The Lord...slow to anger.

This *"fruit of the Holy Spirit"* comes as a result of His influence on our lives. It's the Lord's Personality becoming our personality. Some of us have a bit more of a head start than others, but all of us get the same seeds of the Holy Spirit when we're born again. Cultivating the seeds of this new nature is a process that we yield to. It's not something we must earn or qualify for. Having said that, I'm now going to stretch this point a bit. Look closely at these two verses:

> **1 John 3:2** *"Dear friends, we are God's children **now**; and **it has not yet been made clear what we will become**. We do know that when he appears, **we will be like him**; because **we will see him as he really is**. 3 And **everyone who has this hope in him continues purifying himself**, since God is pure."* CJB

These verses give the Bridal Company three important keys to remember. First, *"**It has not yet been made clear what we will become;**"* meaning, we are only partially aware of what our functions will be in eternity and what our *"Marriage"* with Jesus will actually be like. Second, *"**We do know that when he appears, we will be like him; because we will see him as he really is.**"* This tells us that our Bridal preparation will not be complete until our death or the return of the Lord. It also says, *"we will be like him,"* which tells us the process WILL be completed in due time. The verses connect our Bridal *"completion"* with seeing Jesus as He really is, and they tell us that will not fully occur until we go to be with Him.

Third, *"And everyone who has this hope in him continues purifying himself, since God is pure."* This means, even though our preparation is the responsibility of the Holy Spirit, and even though it's a process, our preparation must include our willing *purification*. We've been purchased with the blood of Jesus. We're not our own. Therefore, with His help, we must actively press toward the mark of holiness and purity to be part of the Bride who has made herself ready. We must clothe ourselves with righteousness by living our lives in agreement with His Word. We're His workmanship, and He'll be faithful to finish what He started, if we stay closely connected to Him.

Perhaps you've read this book and thought, *"I could never be like those people in the Bible."* Or maybe you think you can't be as good as Christians in the Bridal Company I describe. God is looking for a Wife, comprised of *"normal"* but redeemed mankind. Some people resist becoming committed Christians, because they are afraid they can't be *"good enough"* or *"do it"* well enough. They underestimate the power and influence of God. It's not about our ability or good-ness. We're His workmanship. Our responsibility is simply to yield our lives to the Lord in a holy partnership, like a good marriage. God will prepare us, if our hearts are toward Him.

Friends, Jesus is looking for someone just like you to be part of His Bride. You're not too old, you're not too young, you are not too weak, you are not too sinful, and it's not too late. You can be part of the Bridal Company, because He's the one who invited you. Once you begin, He's committed to finish the work that needs to be done in your life. I remind you of the story of my wife who thought she could never be good enough to be *"a Pastor's wife."* If she and I can be part of the Bridal Company of Christ, anyone can do it. The Wedding of the Great

King is open to who-so-ever will come. He'll teach us what He likes, and we'll be like Jesus when we see Him, because we'll see Him as He really is.

If your desire truly is to be part of the Bride of Christ, and if you will submit to His loving guidance, the Lord will prepare you for it. May you receive a deep, personal assurance that you are just what Jesus is looking for. The Holy Spirit will help you to understand what you must release and what you should pursue. As the personal *Friend of the Bridegroom*, the Holy Spirit led you to this book, and He will guide you into all truth. This is the revealed will of God, as proclaimed all throughout the Bible. **Heaven would not be Heaven without you. Jesus loves you, and you're just what He's looking for. By His grace, you'll be part of His Bridal Company forever.**

> **John 16:13** *"But when **He, the Spirit of truth, comes, He will guide you into all truth.** He will not speak on his own; He will speak only what He hears, and **He will tell you what is yet to come.**"* NIV (capitalizations for Holy Spirit pronouns added)

CHAPTER 20:

The Marriage Feast

*Rev. 19:9 "And the angel said, 'Write this: **Blessed are those who are invited to the wedding feast of the Lamb.**' And he added, 'These are true words that come from God.'"* NLT

There's a picture on my office wall, right by my desk. It wouldn't mean much to you if you saw it. I rarely explain why I have it, but it helps me to keep my thoughts focused on things that really matter. The picture is to my right, at eye level. It's an iconic image of two young boys holding cane fishing poles, each with a very small fish at the end of their lines. The boys were both pre-teenagers. The happy youngsters were proudly grinning at me and laughing about their two small fish as I took their picture. I treasure that picture, because I took it the last summer of their lives. You see, both boys had fought long battles with cancer that ended shortly after that fishing trip. They both died before another summer came. Both were twelve years old at the time of their death.

The Angel in Bagel Heaven

It was a magical week, where little bald girls with mouths full of chemo sores could dress up in pretty sun hats and fancy white gloves to have tea parties, while pretending to be elegant southern ladies. Small, one-armed boys in cowboy out-fits could run and have squirt gun fights, without their nervous parents hovering over them. Children with bulging, portable chemo-catheters implanted in their upper chests, could swim in regular lake water, without adults fussing over the potential for germs. Every year we had a local band come for *"The Prom,"* where all of the campers could dress up for the big dance that might be the only one they would ever attend. Our special campers did not pay money to come to camp, because the price of admission was a confirmed diagnosis of cancer.

Camp Fun Times[101] was a special camp where kids with cancer could just be kids for one week each summer. For the other fifty-one weeks, the camp was a state-owned, university supported, educational facility. This amazing one-week camp was started by a passionate woman who loved children and wanted to help them and their families get through the darkest hours of their lives. It was staffed completely with volunteers, and some of the unpaid workers were the same nurses and doctors who treated the children in their fight against cancer. Others were college students and professors on summer break, business people, lawyers, religious leaders, social workers and people from all walks of life. We even had two stunningly beautiful fashion models that the children irreverently named Frick and Frack.

The regular lives of the campers were marked by helpless family members fearfully watching over them as they underwent radical treatments for cancer. Most were used to being over-protected from every potential thing that could possibly affect their already weakened bodies. Some were rendered permanently child-sized, when radiation and chemotherapy that was intended to kill cancer cells, also stopped their body's normal growth. Others were dissected, irrevers-ibly losing limbs, facial features and even their private parts in frantic attempts to defend their lives from the relentless progression of cancer.

---

[101] The name of the camp and the personal names in this story have been changed. Other than these necessary changes, this is an accurate retelling of what actually transpired.

They all came to Camp Fun Times so they could pretend to be "normal" for one week. For that one week, the focus was not on their illness. They just wanted to be with other kids who knew what it was like to live this way. They wanted to experience a little bit of childhood, before it all ran out.

Each year, my eyes were filled with images of laughing children with missing limbs, as they were dropped off by parents showing the effects of endless fear. Excited campers arrived with tiny bodies ravaged from disease and poisonous cancer treatments. Horrible-wonderful images would flood my waking hours as I carefully hid my tears from the campers.

Each year, I would look around knowing that some of the children wouldn't be back the following year, or ever again. I would lie in my bunk at night, begging God to spare the children and eradicate the horrible diseases that were consuming their bodies and the lives of their entire families. While everyone else slept, I would wander the campgrounds in tears, begging God to heal the children. Some were healed, but many died.

The sun was just rising as we sat on the dock in the early morning South Carolina heat. It was the in-between time, when you could still hear frogs and crickets, but the birds remained quiet. The bright yellow corks floated clearly on the still Santee lake water. The boys laughed deeply with unfeigned joy as they simultaneously pulled in two tiny fish with their wooden cane poles. Mark and Jeff, twelve year old boys, barefoot and wearing cut-off jeans, joyously fished on a South Carolina dock in the fading days of their childhood. Like best friends everywhere, they teased each other over whose small fish was the biggest. I was in charge of the fishing dock that morning, and I took the iconic picture of them that now hangs on my office wall. Looking at that picture, you'd never know it was taken the last summer of their lives.

I knew both boys, but I was especially close to Mark, who suffered from various forms of cancer until they ultimately consumed his body. He was one of my regulars each year. He loved to fish, and he became my very special friend.

An unusually small, shy boy, with radiant black skin, he had a short, thin Afro and huge brown eyes. He'd first been diagnosed with cancer at age six. Over time, it got better, then worse, and it finally worked its way into his brain, while simultaneously metastasizing into his bones. Like the other special children at the camp, he came every year to have some "normal" fun while dealing with the ravages of this horrible disease.

Over the years, I also became close to his mom and dad, as I would take Mark on small make-a-wish type adventures throughout the year. They were Christians, and we often prayed for his healing, seeing some periods of brief remission, but the cancer never completely left his body. He was sick and in pain for so many years, that the medicine would no longer stop his pain. His parents used to read him the Psalms every night, and miraculously, the beautiful words would ease his suffering long enough for him to sleep.

The last week of his life, Mark's mother called and said, ***"Pitts, Mark is still in the hospital, and they've told us he's not going to live much longer. We are going to take him home this weekend and let him "pass" at the house with the family around him. If you want to see him again, you better come by the hospital before we take him home."***

Devastated, I prayed with her on the phone and told her I would come by, but I put it off for most of the week.

After all the years of praying for his healing, it was unthinkable to me that Mark was really going to die. Knowing it would be the last time, I delayed going to see him. I knew he was supposed to leave the hospital on Friday to return to their home town, so Thursday morning, I got up and prepared to go. I cried as I showered, thinking about how his long struggle was about to end in death. I ached for the emotional suffering that his young parents and siblings had endured. Resolved, I dressed, but my eyes kept filling with tears as I left the house by myself, planning my drive to the hospital.

My emotions were so unstable that I needed to get myself together before going to the hospital. I pulled into a local bagel place near my house, ***Bagel Heaven***. It was a hole-in-the-wall shop in a small strip center. The entire place, including the kitchen, would have been about the size of a typical dining room and kitchen in an average American house. They had three small tables in the entrance area and one bathroom shared by both sexes.

When I drove up, I sat out front trying to get myself together, and I saw a short, bald man and a woman enter the shop and approach the serving counter. I got out and fell in behind them in line. As each person entered, the door chimed. When I came in, the woman behind the counter looked up, recognized me as a regular and smiled.

Then she said the strangest thing, *"Wow, he looks just like you."*

I looked around, and there was nobody behind me or sitting down. In fact, the only people in the place were me, the short, bald guy, the woman in line between us and the woman working behind the serving counter. I looked the short, bald guy over while I was waiting my turn in line and decided that he looked nothing like me. The man, then the woman, got their orders and left.

When I stepped up to the counter to place my order, the woman asked, *"Where is your brother? He looked just like you."*

I replied, *"Who? The guy that just left?"*

"No, the man who came in with you. He must be your twin brother."

Confused, I said, *"Nobody was with me when I came in."*

"Come on. He looked just like you, and he was dressed just like you."

I said, *"Honestly, I don't have a twin, and nobody came in with me."*

With a sarcastic emphasis, she said, *"Sure, maybe he was your angel?"*

With those words, *"maybe he was your angel,"* every hair on my body stood up, just like they are doing as I write these words. **What a strange thing to say!**

Stunned and confused by her words, I realized she was absolutely convinced that a man who looked like my identical twin brother, dressed exactly like I was, had entered the almost empty Bagel Heaven with me. *What?*

Confused, but now curious, I tried to question her about what she thought she saw. She apparently thought *"my twin brother"* and I were playing some sort of practical joke on her. Quickly, the broad smile on her face was replaced with nervous glances at the restroom door, as if to say, *"I know this is some kind of trick, and he must be hiding in the bathroom."*

Her friendly welcome evaporated completely as I tried to press her for information on what she saw, until she shut down, refusing to comment on the matter any further.

Placing her hand on her hip while scowling at me, she said, *"What do you want?"*

Puzzled at the chain of events and her odd mention of *"my angel,"* I ordered a plain bagel with cream cheese and a coffee and left. Working through my bagel, I considered the whole episode on my way to the hospital. It was VERY odd, but I couldn't make any sense out of it; so I mentally dropped the subject.

When I walked into Mark's hospital room, his mother was on one side of his bed, and his father was across from the bed in a chair. They weren't talking or looking at each other. Mark was laying quietly in his bed with his eyes closed. I took his little hand in mine, and his mother whispered to him that I had come to visit.

His eyes fluttered open and focused on me, and he greeted me, *"Hi Pitts."*

He closed his eyes, and after a little time elapsed, he unexpectedly stopped breathing. I noticed he didn't seem to be breathing, so I put my hand in front of his mouth to confirm and told his dad, *"I think Mark just slipped away."*

His frantic parents called for help, and the staff went into emergency mode, but it was too late. **My face was the last thing he saw on this side of eternity, and my name was the last name he spoke.**

The rest of that day was a blur, but I'm sure we cried over Mark and for each other. If you have never left the empty body of a dead child behind in a hospital, you can't understand how I felt driving away. It seemed like I was betraying the little person who trusted me and his parents to somehow protect him from death. My words to his parents kept playing over and over in my head, *"I think Mark just slipped away."* Even though I knew he was saved and with Jesus, it felt like total loss and total defeat.

A week or so later, the funeral was held and presided over by his uncle. The entire huge, extended family attended, along with many other children with cancer and a lot of the medical staff who had treated Mark over the years.

The preacher had a classic opening to his message that I will never forget. *"Everyone here knew Mark was sick. He's gone now and not sick anymore. Everybody knew the boy loved Jesus and Jesus loved him. I'm sure that he is with Jesus right now, but how about you? Do you know Jesus like Mark did?"*

He then proceeded to give the strongest, most fire and brimstone filled funeral message I have ever heard. Judging by the volume of the wailing and tears, it had tremendous impact on all in attendance.

Time went by, and my life went on. I thought of the boy often, but was comforted in the knowledge of his salvation and the end of his suffering. One day I was reading a story in my Bible, found in Acts 12. It talked about Peter being let out of prison by an angel and going to a house where a prayer meeting was being held. When he knocked on the door, he called to those inside.

A servant girl came to the door and recognized his voice. *"When she recognized Peter's voice, she was so overjoyed she ran back without opening it and exclaimed, 'Peter is at the door!' 'You're out of your mind,' they told her. When she kept insisting that it was so, they said, 'It must be his angel.'"* (Acts 12:14-15 NIV)

I suddenly noticed that they said, *"It must be his angel."*

The thought immediately struck me, *"Why on earth would they think that 'Peter's angel' could be mistaken for Peter and sound like him?"*

Looking in various commentaries on Acts 12, I found that many first century Jews believed that people had **guardian angels** who **not only sounded like them,** but **looked like them!** They were taught that each of us has an angel watching over us, who looks like us. Apparently, the people were more than willing to believe that Peter's guardian angel had appeared at their door, but unwilling to believe Peter had gotten out of jail and showed up himself!

As I sat and thought on these things, I remembered the day Mark died and my odd episode with the *"angel"* in **Bagel Heaven.** I recalled the woman saying that a man who looked just like me, dressed just like me, had come in with me. I remembered her sarcastic words, *"Sure, maybe he was your angel,"* and the power of God once again hit me like electricity. *"Maybe she did see an angel who looked like me, but why?"*

Trying unsuccessfully to make all of the puzzle parts fit, I prayed, asking the Lord what these things meant. God said these words to my heart, *"Pitts, he was just a frightened little boy. He loved you and trusted you. The reason I let the lady see the angel in Bagel Heaven, was to tell you he looked like you. Your face was the last face Mark saw on this side of the grave. When he crossed into eternity, an angel with a face that looked like yours, was the first one he saw when he opened his eyes on the other side."*

It's been over 20 years, and I still feel the presence of God whenever I think about this story. Of course, there is no way to prove that an angel appeared in Bagel Heaven. I didn't even see him myself. And I have no way of knowing for sure if Mark saw the same angel or any angel on the other side of eternity, at the time of his passing. This story is full of conjecture, but it's sacred to me. It struck me as being so kind and so like our loving JESUS to send an angel with a familiar face to welcome a small boy to heaven. After all of these years, I'm still convinced in my own heart that's what happened.

When Mark died, his parents and I felt total defeat. We had prayed faithfully for his healing for years, but he still died from cancer. It was emotionally devastating and heartbreaking. But, in retrospect, I think much of our pain resulted primarily from our lack of understanding. We thought Mark was no longer part of our lives. We tend to think that our loved ones who die become only memories in our past. Biblically, that's a lie. Our loved ones in Christ are waiting for us in our future.

Perhaps you have had a similar experience losing a child or someone close to you after asking God to heal them? It hurts deeply. In our humanity, it is painful to be separated by sickness and death, from those we love. But we need to consider God's perspective. Our loved ones who die in Christ (and babies and young children) are safely transferred into our future. They are safe and well. They are waiting for us with JESUS on the other side. They are not lost to us, just inaccessible for a season until we join them. This perspective is both comforting and based on reality.

The Wedding Feast

I need to back up and tell you one more story that happened the day Mark died. Before I arrived, his mother and her sister were sitting in the hospital room, when Mark suddenly opened his eyes and pointed his finger at something only he could see. He astounded his mother and his aunt by asking, *"Who are all those people, and why are they standing around that big table covered with food?"*

He went on to describe a panoramic scene of a great banquet that was about to take place in his hospital room, with all the guests waiting for him to join them. In the natural realm, he pointed to a chair with a coat hanging on it, as he described the other-worldly images only he could see. At the time, his mother didn't know he was only hours away from death, so she thought him delirious. They told me that story right after his death, later that same day. Then we realized that he had been viewing a feast in eternity that the Lord had prepared for him.

As they described what Mark had seen, it brought to mind a line from King David's Twenty-third Psalm, *"Thou preparest a table before me in the presence of mine enemies."* Perhaps Mark remembered those words that had often been read to him and caught a glimpse of the table God had prepared for him in eternity? He had briefly described a great banquet table, covered with lavish food of every type, surrounded by well-dressed, happy people waiting for him to join them. Perhaps, even while his *"enemies,"* (cancer and death) were still in Mark's *"presence"* on this earth, the Lord allowed him to see what he was really about to victoriously experience?

There's a second scripture that later came to mind. The Bible says that a **wedding feast** will be held for JESUS and those who love Him. *"And the angel said to me, 'Write this: Blessed are those who are invited to the wedding feast of the Lamb.'"* (Rev. 19:9 NLT) Our earthly lives in Christ will be celebrated at *"the wedding feast of the Lamb."* This great banquet is portrayed in Scripture as the consummation of our relationship with JESUS on earth as Christians. Perhaps, Mark was seeing *"the Wedding Feast of the Lamb?"* Possibly, God let him peer briefly beyond the veil, where no demon of cancer or angel of death could keep him from seeing it. God knows what Mark actually saw, but I'm certain he and all of my loved ones in Christ, will be at the Wedding Feast of the Lamb. When my young friend died from cancer, it felt like total defeat. Like Mark, each of us will one day pass from this life to the next. Each of us has been invited to the *"wedding feast of the Lamb."* The Bible says, *"Blessed are those who are invited."* Jesus will come for His Bride, and the wedding party will go with Him to His Father's House. They will gather there along with the redeemed of all the ages. The doors will be shut forever to those who were not born again. Nobody else will be allowed to enter, and nothing will disturb the proceedings as the ceremony begins and the Lord Jesus is joined to the Church as His Bride. Mark accepted the Lord's invitation at a very young age. He lived for the Lord, and when he reached the end of his race, he went to celebrate with Jesus. I have the picture of him and Jeff by my desk to remind me that life is short and it's appointed once for every man to die. As I look at the picture and see Mark's radiant young face, I remember that my days are numbered and they need to count for something.

One day soon, Jesus will return for His Bride. *The Wedding Feast* will occur at the time of His Second Coming. The responsive guests will enter His Father's House; the gates will be shut, and those who have refused the Lord's invitation will be forever barred from entering in. We will gather there along with the redeemed of all the ages. Our coming together with the Lord will then be celebrated at what the Bible calls *"the wedding feast of the Lamb."* This great banquet is portrayed in Scripture as the consummation of our earthly walk as Christians. Maybe it speaks of the thousand-year Millennium or perhaps it represents the start of our eternal future as an endless celebration with Christ. The true nature of this *Wedding Feast* is known only to the Lord, but **the primary objective is our victorious union with Jesus.**

Recently, a good friend of mine, Rick, came to lead a Men's Retreat at our church. He also had come the year before. Many of our regular men and several guests were deeply touched during both retreats. We put him up in a local hotel close to the church. When the retreat concluded, I told my friend I'd come to the hotel to have dinner with him after I dropped by to pay my respects to a couple I knew, holding their wedding reception at the same hotel.

I went to the reception, but the newly married couple didn't make their appearance right away. After a while, I grew uncomfortable waiting for them, because my friend was waiting upstairs for me to take him to dinner. Even though it felt a little awkward bringing someone who was not officially invited, I decided I'd bring him to the reception with me.

About the time we got back downstairs, the bride and groom made their appearance. As soon as they got settled with their food at the head table, we made our way over to offer our congratulations. When the new bride saw my friend, she remembered Rick as our men's speaker. She excitedly jumped to her feet, pointed her finger and said, *"Thank you, brother Rick. Because of your ministry to my husband last year at the Men's Retreat, I'm standing here today as a bride."* I vaguely remembered that the new groom had attended our Retreat the previous year, but I didn't know he'd been so deeply moved. Apparently, right after the Retreat, he'd bought a ring and immediately went to his then girlfriend and proposed.

So, here before us, was a bride in her wedding dress at a wedding banquet, thanking my friend for his ministry and telling him it had changed both of their lives. The setting and her words seemed prophetic to me as she said, *"Because of your ministry...I am standing here as a bride today."* I was immediately struck with the *Living Parable of Marriage* standing right before me and its implications for the Bride of Christ. We were at a wedding banquet that, like every wedding banquet, foreshadows *the Marriage Supper of the Lamb.* As I considered how this story affected the newly married couple, I was deeply stirred by the Lord.

On the great day of the Marriage Supper of the Lamb, we will see those who are there because of our walk with the Lord. Every life that our lives touch for Jesus, will be there. Imagine your own joy when someone jumps to their feet, points at you and says, *"Because you told me about Jesus, I'm here today as part of the Bride of Christ."* We'll also see those who impacted our lives and made it possible for us to be there.

You may not feel you have a fulltime *"ministry,"* but consider those who your life has touched in some way for the Lord. Every dollar we ever give to the work of the Kingdom helps someone to be at the Marriage of the Lamb. Every time we've shared Christ, every time we've stood up as believers, every Biblical truth we share, makes it possible for someone to be with Jesus at the Wedding Feast. **Who will be there because of you?**

There's a special verse about sharing your faith in Jesus, that comes from the very last chapter of the Bible. It reveals a final mandate for the true Bride of Christ.

> **Rev. 22:17** *"The **Spirit and the bride** say, 'Come!' And let him who hears say, 'Come!' Whoever is thirsty, let him **come;** and whoever wishes, **let him take the free gift of the water of life**."* NIV

This shows the Holy Spirit and the Bride of Christ working together in evangelism; *"The Spirit and the Bride say come."* There will be a generation of the Church that uniquely partners with the Holy Spirit to say, *"come."* This invitation will go to every tribe, tongue and nation. The collective voices of the Spirit-empowered Bride will spread throughout the world for the final harvest. There've been individuals in every generation who fulfilled this mandate, but the last generation of the Church will cooperatively fulfill it, as led by the Holy Spirit. *The Bridal Company* will work in a Holy Spirit directed effort for Earth's concluding evangelistic thrust. You and I are called to be part of that.

I wrote this book for serious disciples of Jesus. Its primary purpose is to stir your deep desire toward Him. When I was a teenager, many were asking the questions, *"Why am I here?" "What is the meaning of life?"* I now know that to be part of the Bridal Company of Christ, is why we were created. **You were created by Jesus, to be with Jesus.**[102] **Knowing Jesus is the reason for your life. Soon, He will live in His Holy City with all who love Him.**

The Lord has made His desires very clear. He created us to live with Him in a relationship that can only be compared to a good marriage. Unlike a human

---

[102] Col. 1:16 For *by him all things were created: things in heaven and on earth, visible and invisible, whether thrones or powers or rulers or authorities; **all things were created by him and for him.** 17 He is before all things, and in him all things hold together.* NIV

marriage, this one will last forever. As living men and women, we can understand marriage, but this is only a shadow of the glorious relationship the Lord has in mind for us. When we become Christians, we enter into union with Christ. If we're not His, we are separated from God, for all eternity. There are no "do-overs" for this life, and today is all we've been promised.

I want to encourage you to share the love of Christ when the opportunity presents itself. Someone shared the Gospel with me, and someone shared it with you. As part of the Bridal Company, empowered and delegated as ***Friends of the Bridegroom*** by the Holy Spirit, we need to be inviting people to the Wedding. In the words of John, the beloved Disciple of Jesus Christ, *"The **Spirit and the bride** say, 'Come!'"* It's up to you, guided and anointed by the Holy Spirit, to say, ***"Come."***

In a conventional Jewish or Christian wedding, the bride has the responsibility to invite the guests to the *Marriage*. But in our case, it's *the Bride of Christ* who invites the guests to the *Marriage of the Lamb*. **Who will stand in eternity and point to you as the primary reason they are with the Lord forever? Who will be at the Marriage Supper of the Lamb because you shared your faith with them?**

Perhaps there's someone you know whose soul may be in jeopardy? You may be concerned about where they'll spend eternity. If you are concerned about their relationship with the Lord, it's probably the Holy Spirit prompting you to share your faith in Jesus. The final harvest has begun. Please remember that Jesus is coming soon, and live as if you believe it. Don't let the opportunities we've been given pass you by. You're the Bride who has been given the job of inviting the wedding guests. If you don't invite them, perhaps they will miss Heaven.

May you live each day in the clear light of eternity. May you and all of your friends and loved ones be found at the Wedding Feast of the Lamb. May you be adorned as a beautiful Bride and prepared to live as the Wife of Jesus Christ forever.

CHAPTER 21:

The City of God

Eternity is about God the Father calling Mankind to a Marriage with Jesus. I believe these pages contain the Blueprints of Heaven for your life and for every church and ministry on earth. The plans are contained within teachings on the Bride of Christ. **Churches are charged by God to build and inhabit an eternal city called** *New Jerusalem.* The city residents are collectively revealed in the Old Testament as **the Wife of God** and as **the Bride of Christ** in the New Testament.

> **Rev. 21:2** *"I saw **the Holy City, the new Jerusalem,** coming down out of heaven from God, **prepared as a bride beautifully dressed for her husband.** 3 And I heard a loud voice from the throne saying, 'Now the dwelling of God is with men, and he will live with them. They will be his people, and God himself will be with them and be their God. **9b** Come, I will show you **the bride, the wife of the Lamb.'** 10 And he carried me away in the Spirit to a mountain great and high, and showed me **the Holy City, Jerusalem,** coming down out of heaven from God."* NIV

In the first few months of 1998, we were expecting our twin baby girls, Rebekah and Sara. We didn't know that they were identical at that time, but when we found out that we were having twins, we got VERY excited. We prepared a room for them with two matching beds, two changing tables, and two of every kind of baby thing anyone would ever need. The room was set up with fun wallpaper and all kinds of neat baby decorations. Our other children, Joseph, Courtney and Rachael, were as happy and anxious for the twins to come as Mary and I. Friends gave us many encouraging words about the babies' futures, and we knew they were praying for us as well.

After forty full weeks, our perfect, identical twin girls, Rebekah and Sara Evans, were stillborn on the evening of March 3, 1998. I remember thinking that this couldn't be happening. It was surreal. Surely, after all of the prenatal care and all of the trips to the doctor when they were healthy, the babies weren't gone? But they were. They shared a common umbilical cord that had somehow gotten wrapped around one of them and blocked off, stopping the supply of life to both girls. They gave Mary our new twins, and as she held them and cried, I cried too. I just couldn't bring myself to hold them; but I looked closely at them, and they were perfect little duplicates of each other.

We notified a Pastor friend and his wife about what had happened. They came to the hospital, and together we prayed for the babies to be raised from the dead, but they stayed dead. As his wife comforted Mary, my friend and I walked out into the hall. He said something like this to me: ***"Pitts, this is awful, and I know you're upset; but it almost seems like you're okay with this."*** I looked at him and said the following words that I'll never forget. ***"Brother, at a time like this, it's good to find out that you really believe what you thought you believed."***

You see, even though I didn't expect the sudden loss of our twin baby girls, I knew we'd see them again. For me and Mary, their death was not the end of the story. By that stage of our lives, we knew beyond a shadow of doubt that God was good. **We also knew that the Bible says one day all of the people of God will** live together in the city called *New Jerusalem.* We knew our babies were safe with the Lord in His Eternal City, and we knew we'd join them in the fullness of time. Our hearts were broken, but we knew our babies were home with Jesus.

In the following passages from Revelation, the angel of the Lord showed John a scene from outside of time concerning **the Bride of Christ.**

> **Rev. 21:1** *"Then I saw a new heaven and a new earth, for the first heaven and the first earth had passed away, and there was no longer any sea. 2 I saw **the Holy City, the New Jerusalem,** coming down out of heaven from God, **prepared as a bride beautifully dressed for her husband.**"* NIV

> **Rev. 21:9** *"One of the seven angels who had the seven bowls full of the seven last plagues came and said to me, 'Come, **I will show you the bride, the wife of the Lamb.**' 10 And he carried me away in the Spirit to a mountain great and high, and **showed me the Holy City, Jerusalem,** coming down out of heaven from God."* NIV

What remains after heaven and earth are made new, is **JESUS** and a City called **New Jerusalem, dressed as a Bride for her Husband**. Of course, **Jesus is the Lamb of God**. The angel of the Lord identified **the Lamb's Wife as the occupants of the Holy City**. The Lord was saying that **the Bride of Christ is a Bridal Company**, made up of the redeemed from every generation, living together in the Holy City called New Jerusalem. These passages reveal God's ultimate plan to live with you and the saints of all the ages, in a collective city He calls His Bride.

So you don't get the wrong impression of me and my wife, I want to revisit the loss of our twins. We're not some sort of super-Christians who can just lose our children and not be deeply hurt. After they died, we returned to the house without them. Leaving our two little girls in that cold hospital was the hardest thing we've ever done. Mary had to take medication for a while, and I didn't sleep much for the next three months. We wept together often and comforted each other the best we could. While Mary was recovering, her mother came to stay with us to help take care of her and the kids. Needless to say, the atmosphere in our house was pretty grim at the time. We'd always been a joyful group, but the loss of the twins had deeply grieved the entire family and made our house a very sad, quiet place.

On the third day after Mary's mother came, I was in the kitchen making myself something to eat. There was a stereo that, prior to the loss of the twins, had played Christian worship music twenty-four hours a day. I looked at the stereo and decided that God still was worthy of our worship, so I turned it on and turned it up loud. Our two girls, Courtney and Rachael, came into the kitchen to see what was going on. At that moment, a song called *"We Will Dance"* began to play. The words are about the *City of New Jerusalem*. As the phrase *"We will dance on the streets that are golden, the Glorious Bride and the great Son of Man..."* started to play, I grabbed my remaining daughters by their hands, and we began to dance with all of our might.

We were in the kitchen singing and dancing through tears, but in our hearts, we were dancing before the Lord with our twins in the *City of New Jerusalem*. About that time, my mother-in-law came down to investigate the loud music. When she saw what was going on, she smiled and said, *"I think everything is going to be fine here, so it's time for me to go home."*

Shortly after that, Mary and I were talking. She felt like a transition had happened to our family, and now we were all living with a bigger investment in eternity than we previously had. We decided that we should live out the remainder of our lives for Jesus, in the light of what makes sense for eternity. Our response was to leave our old lives and attend Bible School in preparation for ministry.

The loss of the twins is actually what *"led us"* into training for full time ministry. The Lord didn't kill our babies, but our reaction to their deaths allowed us to step into our destiny. **When trouble comes, you can pull away from God or draw near to Him. Jesus is always the solution and never the problem. Your response determines your destiny.**

Perhaps you've lost a baby through miscarriage or disease? If they were unborn, or under the age of accountability, they are waiting for you with Jesus. Or perhaps you've lost someone else close to you who was a committed Christian? They, too, are waiting for you in the *City of New Jerusalem.* They're not just part of your past; those who die in the Lord become part of our future. **Together, we'll be joined into the Wife of the Lamb, living in the Bridal Company known as New Jerusalem.** Our job is to prepare on earth for our future as citizens of that eternal city.

Friends, there's a real city of God, where all of the people of God will live forever. It's not a myth, and it's not something misguided men made up to comfort grieving parents. It's called the *City of New Jerusalem,* because it points to the *Lord's Wife, Israel,* and it provides the eternal dwelling place for the *Bride of Christ.* The occupants are made up of those from *"every tribe, tongue and nation"* who love God and lived their lives according to His purposes. Nothing on this earth compares to it. Everyone you've ever known who served God will be there. All of the stillborn babies and all of the aborted babies will be there too. Seeing that this is true, we ought to do everything we can to get there, and take as many people with us as we can.

You should take comfort in what I've written, but these things also carry a challenge of responsibility. **The Bride of Christ is a corporate Bride. The Bride who has made herself ready (Rev. 19:7), speaks of our shared responsibility for preparation as a Bridal Company. We must reset our vision from strictly personal preparation, to concern for the preparation of every believer.** That implies a shared responsibility for you. My wife and I have pledged our lives for preparation of the Bride of Christ. I want to ask you to do the same. May we live in such a way as to bring multitudes to New Jerusalem. Friends, **Jesus and I are looking forward to seeing you there and living with you forever.**

"He who testifies to these things says,
'Yes, I am coming soon.' Amen. Come, Lord Jesus.
The grace of the Lord Jesus be with God's people. Amen."
Revelation 22:20-21 NIV

Addendum 1:

Hebraic Marriage Customs

1 Cor. 10:11 *"Now **these things were done as an example; and were put down in writing for our teaching,** on whom the last days have come."* BBE

My intent with this Addendum is to present an overview of the Hebraic Marriage Customs in reasonable order. A few of the customs appear below without foundational scripture support, but I include verses to make the custom more memorable. Before presenting the list of Customs and Scripture References, there are a few things I want to mention.

There is no central authority concerning Jewish Wedding customs, nor is there general agreement as to which customs (if any) are connected to which scriptures. There are many different forms of Judaism, and Jewish customs range over almost 4,000 years. Traditional marriage practices were often different during different periods of time. Jewish and Christian interpretations of Biblical practices often vary on their meanings. Frequently, when looking at these marriage customs, Jews do not agree with Christians on their symbolism, Jews often disagree with other Jews, and Christians often disagree with other Christians.

This list is not intended to be exhaustive; it is a compilation that I am comfortable with. I have attempted to include only the customs that are most commonly mentioned. Some of the verses I used below require additional explanation to make the connections with the customs more obvious. Additional explanations are presented in some of the chapters. Please keep in mind that we are compiling a list of practices that were used in different eras. The sequence is impossible to determine, and the numbers used below are included just to make a more orderly presentation of the material. **Finally, please remember that not every custom could have been used in every Jewish wedding.**

1.   **Marriage in Bible times was initiated by the father of the groom.**
     Matt. 22:2 *"The kingdom of heaven is **like a king who prepared a wedding banquet for his son.**"* NIV

2.   **An agent could be used to search for the bride and mediate. This agent was referred to as a matchmaker (*shadkhan*), sometimes known as *"the Friend of the Bridegroom."***
     John 3:29 *"He that hath the bride is the bridegroom: but **the friend of the bridegroom**, which standeth and heareth him, rejoiceth greatly because of the bridegroom's voice: this my joy therefore is fulfilled."* KJV

     2 Cor 11:2 *"For I am jealous over you with godly jealousy: for I have espoused you to one husband, that I may present you as a chaste virgin to Christ."* KJV

3.   **A search would be made for a suitable candidate to be the bride.**
     Esther 2:2 *"Then the king's personal attendants proposed, '**Let a search be made** for beautiful young virgins for the king.'"* NIV

4. After locating the potential bride, her consent and the consent of her family would be sought. The consent of the bride had to be given for the agreement to be valid.

    Gen. 24:58 *"So they called Rebekah and asked her, 'Will you go with this man?' 'I will go,' she said."* NIV

5. When a tentative agreement for marriage had been reached, the two families would get together and negotiate the Bride Price. The amount of the Bride Price would reflect the relative value the groom and his family placed on the potential bride as a wife.

    Heb. 9:15 *"For this reason Christ is the mediator of a **new covenant**, that those who are called may receive the promised eternal inheritance — now that **he has died as a ransom** to set them free from the sins committed under the first covenant."* NIV

6. If the bride and her family agreed to the marriage, a marriage covenant (*ketubah*) would be drawn up, explaining the nature of the agreement.

    Jer. 31:31 *"'The time is coming,' declares the Lord, 'when I will make **a new covenant** with the house of Israel and with the house of Judah. 32 **It will not be like the covenant I made with their forefathers** when I took them by the hand to lead them out of Egypt, because they broke my covenant, though **I was a husband to them,' declares the Lord.**"* NIV

    Matt. 26:28 *"For this is My blood of **the [new and better] covenant**, which [ratifies the agreement and] is being poured out for many [as a substitutionary atonement] for the forgiveness of sins."* [Ex 24:6-8.] AMP

7. When they had settled on a Bride Price, they sealed the agreement
   with a glass of wine that was known as "the Cup of Acceptance."
   Luke 22:20 *"In the same way, after the supper **he took the cup,**
   saying, "**This cup** is the new covenant in my blood, which is
   poured out for you."* NIV

8. A valuable gift or coin was given to the bride to secure the transaction. This is called a "*mohar,*" which is a cash gift promised in the
   marriage contract by the groom to the bride. If she accepted the gift
   before witnesses, this would attest to her willing agreement.
   Gen. 24:53 *"Then **the servant brought out gold and silver**
   jewelry and articles of clothing and gave them to Rebekah; he
   also gave costly gifts to her brother and to her mother." NIV

9. The groom would pay the Bride Price.
   John 10:17b *"**I lay down my life** — only to take it up again. 18*
   No one takes it from me, but I lay it down of my own accord." NIV

   John 19:30 *"When he had received the drink ("wine", TEV),*
   *Jesus said, '**It is finished.**' With that, he bowed his head and gave*
   up his spirit." NIV

   "*it is finished*" NT:5055 teleo (tel-eh'-o); **to discharge a debt.**

10. After the Bride Price had been paid, the two would be officially
    betrothed or espoused. "*Kiddushin*" is the betrothal stage of mar-
    riage that precedes the nuptials.

2 Cor. 11:2 *"For I am jealous over you with godly jealousy: for* ***I have espoused you to one husband***, *that I may present you as a chaste virgin to Christ."* KJV

11. The purchased and waiting bride was referred to as *"One Who Is Bought with a Price."*

    1 Cor. 6:20 *"For* ***ye are bought with a price****: therefore glorify God in your body, and in your spirit, which are God's."* KJV

12. Following the betrothal, the groom would sometimes give the bride ten silver coins as a bridal gift or token of their betrothal, which she would later make into a garland or necklace for the actual wedding ceremony.

    Luke 15:8 *"Or suppose a woman has* ***ten silver coins*** *and loses one. Does she not light a lamp, sweep the house and search carefully until she finds it? 9 And when she finds it, she calls her friends and neighbors together and says, 'Rejoice with me; I have found my lost coin.'"* NIV

13. After the marriage covenant was settled and the betrothal had begun, the groom would make a formal speech to his bride. *"I am going to go prepare a place for you, and when it is done I will return and get you. Then you will live with me as my wife."*

    John 14:2 *"In my Father's house are many mansions: if it were not so, I would have told you.* ***I go to prepare a place for you. 3 And if I go and prepare a place for you, I will come again, and receive you unto myself; that where I am, there ye may be also."*** KJV

14. The groom would then go back to his father's house and build an addition onto the house for himself and his future bride. *Only the father of the groom could give final approval for the completion of the addition, and his approval would signal that the day of the wedding had come. He would then say, "Go and get your bride."*
John 14:2 *"In my Father's house are **many rooms**; if it were not so, I would have told you. I am going there to prepare a place for you."* NIV

   Mark 13:32 *"No one knows about that day or hour, not even the angels in heaven, nor the Son, but **only the Father**."* NIV

15. The waiting bride was responsible for her own preparation while the groom worked on their new home.
Rev. 19:7 *"Let us rejoice and be glad and give him glory! For the wedding of the Lamb has come, and **his bride has made herself ready**."* NIV

16. The future bride was expected to submit to traditional purification by immersion and washings. A *"mikveh"* is a pool of water used for purposes of ritual purification.
Rom. 6:3 *"Or don't you know that all of us who were **baptized** into Christ Jesus were baptized into his death?"* NIV

   Eph. 5:25 *"Husbands, love your wives, just as Christ loved the church and gave himself up for her 26 to make her holy, **cleansing her by the washing with water** through the word."* NIV

17. The bride was expected to give her marriage plans for her future husband, her undistracted devotion.

    Mark 12:30 *"Love the Lord your God with all your heart and with all your soul and with all your mind and with all your strength."* NIV

18. The bride was responsible for making or acquiring her Bridal Garments.

    Rev. 19:7 *"Let us rejoice and be glad and give him glory! For the wedding of the Lamb has come, and his bride has made herself ready. 8 **Fine linen, bright and clean, was given her to wear.**"* NIV

19. It was also common for the bride to acquire jewelry for the wedding.

    Isa. 61:10 *"...as **a bride adorneth herself with her jewels.**"* KJV

20. The bride would gather her dowry to be presented at the wedding.

    Rev. 4:10 *"The twenty-four elders fall down before him who sits on the throne, and worship him who lives for ever and ever. **They lay their crowns** before the throne."* NIV

21. The bride had to remain prepared at all times for the coming of the groom.

    Luke 12:40 *"**You also must be ready,** because the Son of Man will come at an hour when you do not expect him."* NIV

22. After the father of the groom approved that the preparations were complete, they would blow a *"shofar"* to announce the wedding and

notify the bridal party that the groom was coming. A *shofar* is a trumpet, traditionally made from a ram's horn.

1 Thess. 4:16 *"For the Lord himself will come down from heaven, with a loud command, with the voice of the archangel and with **the trumpet call of God**, and the dead in Christ will rise first."* NIV

23. **The arrival of the groom was always sudden and unexpected.**
    Rev. 16:15 *"Behold, **I come like a thief!** Blessed is he who stays awake and keeps his clothes with him, so that he may not go naked and be shamefully exposed."* NIV

24. **The guests had to be ready to go out and meet the groom.**
    1 Thess. 4:17 *"Then we which are alive and remain shall be caught up together with them in the clouds, **to meet the Lord** in the air: and so shall we ever be with the Lord."* KJV

25. **The groom and all of the wedding guests would then go to the house of the bride's father at midnight.**
    Matt. 25:6 *"**At midnight** the cry rang out: '**Here's the bridegroom! Come out to meet him!**'"* NIV

26. **As the groom and his wedding party would approach, the bridal party would light oil lamps and come out to meet them.**
    Matt. 25:1 *"At that time the kingdom of heaven will be **like ten virgins who took their lamps and went out to meet the bridegroom.**"* NIV

27. The groom would "*Steal His Bride*" while her father turned his back, in a conspiracy that has become known as a friendly kidnapping.

    Judges 21:20 *"So they instructed the Benjamites, saying, 'Go and hide in the vineyards 21 and watch. When the girls of Shiloh come out to join in the dancing, then rush from the vineyards and each of you **seize a wife** from the girls of Shiloh and go to the land of Benjamin... 23 So that is what the Benjamites did. While the girls were dancing, **each man caught one and carried her off to be his wife.**'"* NIV

    Rev. 16:15 *"Behold, **I come like a thief!** Blessed is he who stays awake and keeps his clothes with him, so that he may not go naked and be shamefully exposed."* NIV

28. The entire combined wedding party would return to the groom's father's house and gather in the central courtyard for the final ceremony and marriage supper.

    Matt. 25:10 *"And while they went to buy, **the bridegroom came;** and they that were ready went in with him to the marriage: and **the door was shut.**"* KJV

    Rev. 19:9 *"Then the angel said to me, 'Write: **"Blessed are those who are invited to the wedding supper of the Lamb!"**'"* NIV

29. To be invited to a wedding was an honor that was not to be refused. The more noble the bride and groom, the greater the honor. To refuse to come to the wedding of a King or a Prince in Israel was unthinkable.

Matt. 22:2 *"The kingdom of heaven is like a king who prepared a wedding banquet for his son. 3 He sent his servants to those who had been invited to the banquet to tell them to come, but **they refused to come.**"* NIV

30. The invited wedding guests were referred to as *"the Children of the Bridechamber."*
    Mark 2:19 *"And Jesus said unto them, Can **the children of the bridechamber** fast, while the bridegroom is with them? As long as they have the bridegroom with them, they cannot fast."* KJV

31. The doors of the father's compound would be shut, so no more guests could enter and disturb the marriage proceedings.
    Matt. 25:10 *"But while they were on their way to buy the oil, the bridegroom arrived. The virgins who were ready went in with him to the wedding banquet. And **the door was shut.**"* NIV

32. The bride places a veil over her face before approaching the groom. The groom lifts the veil and verifies her face, making sure he is about to marry the right woman.
    Gen. 24:64 *"Rebekah also looked up and saw Isaac. She got down from her camel 65 and asked the servant, 'Who is that man in the field coming to meet us?' 'He is my master,' the servant answered. So **she took her veil and covered herself.**"* NIV

33. The groom also begins to wear a prayer shawl called a *"tallith"* on his wedding day, just as God was supposed to have been seen wearing one at His wedding with Israel at Mount Sinai.
    Ps. 104:2 *"He wraps himself in light as with a garment;"* NIV

34. The bride and groom are treated as a king and queen on their wedding day with an assortment of customs, including special head coverings like crowns and sitting in special chairs that are then elevated by the guests after the ceremony.

    Ps. 45:13 *"The **royal daughter** is all glorious within the palace; Her clothing is woven with gold. 14 **She shall be brought to the King** in robes of many colors;"* NKJV

35. After the actual ceremony, there would be a series of blessings that were sealed at the end with a cup of wine. The seven blessings are known as *"Sheva Berakhot"* or *"Sheva Bachot."*

    1 Cor. 10:16 *"The **cup of blessing** which we bless, is it not the communion of the blood of Christ? The bread which we break, is it not the communion of the body of Christ?"* KJV

36. The bride and groom would enter the Bridechamber tent that had been set up to consummate the wedding. Their entry into the marriage chamber had to be witnessed by other people. This traditional use of a Bridechamber tent was later reduced to the *"huppah"* ceremony. A *huppah* is a bridal canopy.

    Gen. 24:67 *"And Isaac brought her into **his mother Sarah's tent**, and **took Rebekah, and she became his wife;** and he loved her: and Isaac was comforted after his mother's death."* KJV

    Song. 1:4 *"Draw me, we will run after thee: **the king hath brought me into his chambers:** we will be glad and rejoice in thee, we will remember thy love more than wine: the upright love thee."* KJV

37. **The Friend of the Bridegroom** would stand at the door to the Bridechamber listening for the voice of the bridegroom and announce when the marriage had finally been consummated.
John 3:29 *"He that hath the bride is the bridegroom: but* *the friend of the bridegroom, which standeth and heareth him,* *rejoiceth greatly because of the **bridegroom's voice**: this my joy* *therefore is fulfilled."* KJV

38. *The Friend of the Bridegroom* would also produce proof of the union in the form of a bloodstained sheet that had been stained during that first marital intercourse. This wedding sheet would be preserved for the future as *proof of the bride's virtue*.
Deut. 22:17 *"'...But **here is the proof** that my daughter was* *a virgin; **look at the bloodstains on the wedding sheet!**'...19* *Moreover, **she will continue to be his wife**, and he can never* *divorce her as long as he lives."* GNT

39. At almost all modern weddings, they break a glass. Some think this is an ancient custom done in memory of the destruction of Solomon's Temple. Specifically, some say that Solomon had a special gate built out of glass for bridegrooms to enter the Temple, and this was destroyed by Babylon, so that is why a glass is broken.
2 Kings 25:8b *"Babylon, came to Jerusalem. 9 **He set fire to*** ***the temple of the Lord, the royal palace and all the houses*** ***of Jerusalem. Every important building he burned down.** 10* *The whole Babylonian army, under the commander of the imperial guard, broke down the walls around Jerusalem."* NIV

40. **The Wedding Feast would begin and be celebrated for seven days that speak of the seven days of creation. Afterward, the bride and groom would begin their new life together.**

    Rev. 19:9 *"And the angel said to me, 'Write this: **Blessed are those who are invited to the wedding feast of the Lamb.**' And he added, 'These are true words that come from God.'"* NLT

    Rev. 21:2 *"I saw **the Holy City, the new Jerusalem, coming down out of heaven from God, prepared as a bride beautifully dressed for her husband.**"* NIV

To conclude this Addendum, I want to remind the reader that this list of Jewish Wedding Customs and the scriptures I used to support the Customs, are not intended to be complete or universally agreed upon. My sources are not noted in this chapter, because I reference and footnote them in other places. This is my personal list, compiled over many years of teaching on the Bride of Christ. As I mentioned above, many of these customs are discussed in more detail in the book chapters.

I want to point you to two more Bible verses concerning marriage, from the book of Ephesians. Paul said, *"For this reason a man will leave his father and mother and be united to his wife, and the two will become one flesh. This is a profound mystery — but I am talking about Christ and the church."* (Eph. 5:31-32 NIV) Paul was really telling us that, for those who have eyes to see, marriage is a God-given mystery that can teach us many things about our relationship with Jesus. In other words, we should look at marriage as an example that the Lord uses to explain spiritual concepts about our relationship with Him. **Since the entire Bible is about God's search for a relationship with mankind, that means we are on very solid theological ground in trying to examine scripture verses and connect them to weddings and wedding customs for clues on how the Lord wants to relate to us.**

Addendum 2:

Seven Wedding Blessings (Sheva Bachot)

1. *Blessed art Thou, O Lord our God, King of the universe who hast created the fruit of the vine.*

2. *Blessed art Thou, O Lord our God, King of the universe who hast created all things for His glory.*

3. *Blessed art Thou, O Lord our God, King of the universe, creator of man.*

4. *Blessed art Thou, O Lord our God, King of the universe who hast made man in His image, after his likeness, and hast prepared for him, out of his very self, a perpetual fabric. Blessed art Thou, O Lord, creator of man.*

5. *May she who was barren be exceedingly glad and rejoice when her children are united in her midst in joy. Blessed art Thou, O Lord, who makes Zion joyful through her children.*

6. *O make these beloved companions greatly rejoice even as Thou didst rejoice over Thy creation in the Garden of Eden as of old. Blessed art Thou, O Lord, who makest bridegroom and bride to rejoice.*

7. *Blessed art Thou, O Lord our God, King of the universe who hast created joy and gladness, bridegroom and bride, mirth and exultation, pleasure and delight, love, brotherhood, peace and fellowship. Soon may there be heard in the cities of Judah and in the streets of Jerusalem, the voice of joy*

and gladness, the voice of the bridegroom and the voice of the bride, the jubilant voice of bridegrooms from their canopies, and of youths from their feasts of song. Blessed art Thou, O Lord, who makest the bridegroom to rejoice with the bride.

Addendum II was compiled directly from Maurice Lamm's, *The Jewish Way in Love and Marriage* (Middle Village: Jonathan David Publishers, Inc., 1980), 223-227.

SUGGESTED READING

Arthur, Kay. <u>Israel My Beloved.</u> Eugene, Harvest House Publishers, 1996.

Hill, S.J. <u>Burning Desire.</u> Orlando, Relevant Books, 2005.

Kaplan, Rabbi Aryeh, <u>Made in Heaven.</u> New York, Moznaim Publishing Corporation, 1983.

Lamm, Maurice, <u>The Jewish Way in Love and Marriage.</u> Middle Village, Jonathan David Publishers, Inc. 1980.

Taylor, Wade E. <u>The Secret of the Stairs.</u> Salisbury Center, Pinecrest Publications, 2000.

GENERAL BIBLIOGRAPHY

Anderson, Ken. Where to Find It in the Bible. Carmel, Thomas Nelson Publishers, 1996.

Arthur, Kay. With an Everlasting Love. Eugene, Harvest House Publishers, 1995.

_____. Israel My Beloved. Eugene, Harvest House Publishers, 1996.

Barker, Kenneth L. & John R. Kohlenberger III. NIV Bible Commentary on the Old Testament. Grand Rapids, Zondervan Publishing House, 1994.

Cohen, Abraham. Everyman's Talmud. New York, Schocken Books, 1949.

Dimont, Max I. Jews, God and History. New York, Simon & Schuster, 1962.

Edersheim, Alfred. Bible History Old Testament. Grand Rapids, William B. Erdmann Publishing Co., 1977.

_____. The Life and Times of Jesus The Messiah. New York, Longmans, Green, and Co., 1915.

_____. Sketches of Jewish Social Life in the Days of Christ. London, The Religious Track Society, 1908.

Eisenberg, Ronald L. The JPS Guide to Jewish Traditions. Philadelphia, The Jewish Publication Society, 2004.

Freeman, James M. Manners & Customs of the Bible. New Kensington, Whitaker House, 1996.

Fruchtenbaum, Arnold G. The Footsteps of the Messiah. San Antonio, Ariel Press, 2004.

Gesenius, W. L. Gesenius Hebrew-Chaldee Lexicon of the Old Testament. Grand Rapids: Baker Book House, 1979.

Gross, David C. & Esther R., Under the Wedding Canopy, Love and Marriage in Judaism. New York, Hippocrene Books, Inc., 1996.

Halley, Henry H. Halley's Bible Handbook. 24th ed., Grand Rapids, Zondervan Publishing House, 1965.

Hertz, J.H., ed. The Pentateuch and Haftorahs. London, Soncino Press, 1952.

Hill, S.J. Burning Desire. Orlando, Relevant Books, 2005.

Kaiser, Walter C. Jr., Peter H. Davids, F.F. Bruce, Manfred T. Brauch. Hard Sayings of the Bible One Volume Edition. Downers Grove, IVP Academic, 1996.

Kaplan, Rabbi Aryeh, Made in Heaven. New York, Moznaim Publishing Corporation, 1983.

Keener, Craig S. The IVP Bible Background Commentary on the New Testament. Downers Grove, Intervarsity Press, 1993.

Kent, Wilfred R. The Greatest Love Story...Ever Told. Pretoria, TWM International Publishers, 1995.

Laan, Ray Vander. That the World May Know. Video Series, Colorado Springs, Focus on the Family, 1996.

Lamm, Maurice, The Jewish Way in Love and Marriage, Middle Village, Jonathan David Publishers, Inc. 1980.

Levitt, Zola. A Christian Love Story. Self-Published, 1978.

Morlock, Howard. Jewish Faith and the New Covenant. Van Nuys, Rock of Israel, 1980.

Neusner, Jacob, A Midrash Reader. Minneapolis, Fortress Press, 1990.

Schurer, Emil. A History of The Jewish People in the Time of Jesus Christ. New York, Schocken Books, 1961.

Steinberg, Milton. Basic Judaism. San Diego, Harcourt Brace, 1947.

Stern, David H. Jewish New Testament Commentary. Clarksville, Jewish New Testament Publications, 1992.

Taylor, Wade E. The Secret of the Stairs. Salisbury Center, Pinecrest Publications, 2000.

Unger, Merrill F. Unger's Bible Handbook. Chicago: Moody Press, 1965.

Unknown. Heroes of the Faith. Tulsa, Harrison House, 1996.

Willmington, Harold L. Willmington's Bible Handbook. Wheaton, Tyndale House Publishers, 1997.

PC STUDY BIBLE REFERENCES

Adam Clarke's Commentary. Biblesoft, Inc. Version 4.2. CD-ROM, 2007.

Easton's Bible Dictionary. Biblesoft, Inc. Version 4.2. CD-ROM, 2007.

Fausset's Bible Dictionary. Biblesoft, Inc. Version 4.2. CD-ROM, 2007.

International Standard Bible Encyclopaedia. Biblesoft, Inc. Version 4.2. CD-ROM, 2007.

Jamieson, Fausset, and Brown Commentary. Biblesoft, Inc. Version 4.2. CD-ROM, 2007.

Keil and Delitzsch Commentary on the Old Testament. New Updated Edition, Biblesoft, Inc.Version 4.2. CD-ROM, 2007.

Nelson's Illustrated Bible Dictionary. Biblesoft, Inc. Version 4.2. CD-ROM, 2007.

New Exhaustive Strong's Concordance with Expanded Greek-Hebrew Dictionary. Biblesoft, Inc. Version 4.2. CD-ROM, 2007.

Smith's Bible Dictionary. Biblesoft, Inc. Version 4.2. CD-ROM, 2007.

The New Unger's Bible Dictionary. Biblesoft, Inc. Version 4.2. CD-ROM, 2007.

PERSONAL INTERVIEWS

Brown, Michael L., Interview. September 6, 2008.

Gilfillan, Berin, Interview. August 11, 2008.

Morgan, Howard, Interview. October 22, 2008.

Reinstein, Joshua, Interview. August 7, 2008.

Taylor, Wade E., Interview. August 3, 2008.

CPSIA information can be obtained at www.ICGtesting.com
Printed in the USA
BVOW06s2229160716

455832BV00033B/528/P